No Nonsense Gardening Guide™

Using Annuals & Perennials

By the Editors of Garden Way Publishing

D1403229

Longmeadow Press

USING ANNUALS AND PERENNIALS

Copyright © 1990 by Storey Communications, Inc.

Some material for this book has been adapted from *Successful Perennial Gardening* by Lewis and Nancy Hill (Garden Way Publishing). Used by permission.

No Nonsense Gardening Guide is a trademark controlled by Longmeadow Press.

ISBN: 0-681-40966-5

Printed in the United States of America

0 9 8 7 6 5 4 3 2 1

Prepared for Longmeadow Press by Storey Communications, Inc.

President: M. John Storey
Executive VP, Administration: Martha M. Storey
Publisher: Thomas Woll
Series Editor: Benjamin Watson

Cover and inside design by Leslie Morris Noyes
Edited by Nicholas Noyes
Production by Carol Jessop, Joan Genova, Judy Eliason, and Nancy Lamb
Illustrations by Mallory Lake and Judy Eliason

The name Garden Way Publishing is licensed to Storey Communications, Inc, by Garden Way, Inc.

Cover photograph © Madelaine Gray

Contents

THE NO NONSENSE LIBRARY

NO NONSENSE GARDENING GUIDES

Flowering Houseplants
The Successful Vegetable Garden
Using Annuals & Perennials
Landscaping for Beauty
Herbs the Year Round
The Weekend Gardener

OTHER NO NONSENSE GUIDES

Car Guides
Career Guides
Cooking Guides
Financial Guides
Health Guides
Legal Guides
Parenting Guides
Photography Guides
Real Estate Guides
Study Guides
Success Guides
Wine Guides

Chapter 1

Annuals Versus Perennials: The Benefits of Each

The Benefits of Annuals

One of the best rites of spring has to be the "annual" expedition, sallying forth to flower stands to select just the right annual plants to dress up window boxes, accent borders, and tuck in around the perennials, the shrubs, and, yes, even the vegetables. Every year there's something different to catch your eye, to lead you in a new direction of color or design. Some plants, though, are old favorites, like friends just waiting for you to bring them home and put them where they belong. The reward for just a few hours of selection and preparation is instantaneous. You can stand back after the work is done and see the fruits of your labor: fresh new plants, often with dashes of color, amid the emerging greenery. This overnight change is the quickest, most visible sign that spring has truly arrived.

By definition, an annual is a plant that develops from seed, flowers, and produces more seed before dying, all in the period of one year. Other plants we commonly regard as annuals — in fact often described as "treated as annuals" — are really just tender perennials native to areas with a warm climate.

Annual plants offer the closest thing to instant gratification in gardening. Most are easy to grow: the fact that they are in the ground only temporarily means that they have shallow root systems that require less bed preparation than perennials. Further, annuals need little regular maintenance beyond weeding and picking the faded blossoms to maintain and/or increase flowering. They have a long period of bloom and bloom more abundantly the more they are cut, features which make them the mainstay of a good cutting garden. Annual plants come in a rainbow of colors, offering just the right look for nearly any location imaginable. Their diverse shapes, sizes, and textures add to the limitless possibilities.

Annuals are available to suit nearly any location, from shady spots to sunny areas. Certain annuals will thrive in sandy soil while others will be just right in rich loam. Properly spaced and matched to their environment and climate, most annuals require only a bit of fertilizer and occasional checks for disease or insects, thriving with a minimum of fuss.

Getting started with annual gardening requires only a relatively small financial investment to provide a nearly instant payoff in beautifying any area. For the beginning gardener, the fact that the plants are set in anew every year means that landscape designs and color schemes may be changed from year to year as experience, need, or taste dictates. Every gardening season offers the potential to repeat a stunning success, make dramatic improvements, or create a complete change of scenery.

The Benefits of Perennials

From studying the new garden catalogs in mid-January, to tucking in the plants with mulch just before the winter snows arrive, many gardeners derive enormous pleasure from their perennial flowers. As soon as the snow melts in the spring they hurry to the gardens to discover which plants are peeping through the wet earth after their winter hibernation. With the first spring shower, many that had seemed dead on first inspection suddenly sprout green buds, and the gardener knows that more surprises will appear each day until the cycle of the seasons brings winter once again.

It is this quality of metamorphosis that attracts gardeners to perennials. The annual flowers that grow, bloom, produce seed, and die in the same year are lovely, colorful, and predictable throughout the summer. Herbaceous perennials, on the other hand, are fascinating because most bloom for only short periods and seldom look the same two days in a row, or two years in succession. Early morning walks reward you with a changing display of blossoms and an endless variation of plant textures, heights, and fragrances. You wait expectantly to see if the new hybrid iris you splurged on last fall will be as spectacular as the catalog description promised, or if the blooms of the peony that were disappointingly small last summer will improve this year.

Sometimes gardeners wonder, nonetheless, why they spend their summers digging, planting, moving plants from place to place, feeding, and spraying while others swim, boat, play tennis and golf, or relax in a hammock. Perennial gardening isn't always fun. In fact, one gardener has described the struggle with soil, weeds, bugs, and diseases as the "war of the (prim)roses."

The desire to garden, and the pleasure it imparts, no doubt has something to do with the challenge of winning that war, and creating beauty in a spot where only grass and weeds would otherwise be found. It also provides exercise, lovely bouquets, and a good excuse to be outdoors. But the root of this motivation goes deeper: In working with the soil, you join a long procession of humanity tied to the cycle of planting and harvest since the beginning of time.

Many of our most common perennial plants were imported by immigrants or by returning American missionaries and tourists. Others were discovered by professional horticulturists who visited foreign lands especially to seek new species of plant life. Some imports felt so much at home in this country that they quickly became unappreciated weeds. The common daisy, dandelion, devil's paintbrush, tansy, and many others arrived as garden flowers or medicinal herbs, but rapidly spread throughout the countryside. We've heard that the walled garden got its start in this country when a colonist became suspicious and built a stone wall around his wife's flower garden to keep the plants from spreading into his fields. Not all garden perennials are immigrants, of course. Some were native to North America's fields and woods. Wildflowers such as the lady's slipper, bee balm, and mertensia were admired by the early settlers and transplanted into their yards and gardens.

A great many of today's popular perennials bear little resemblance to those our ancestors grew, due to the work of amateur and professional horticulturists. Dedicated hybridizers have created thousands of new peony, iris, lily, *Hemerocallis*, chrysanthemum, delphinium, and other varieties now available in garden centers and nurseries, or through mail-order catalogs.

Planting Zone Map

Approximate Range of Average Annual Mimimum Temperature for Each Zone

ZONE 1	BELOW -50°F
ZONE 2	-50° TO -40°
ZONE 3	-40° TO -30°
ZONE 4	-30° TO -20°
ZONE 5	-20° TO -10°
ZONE 6	-10° TO 0°
ZONE 7	0° TO 10°
ZONE 8	10° TO 20°
ZONE 9	20° TO 30°
ZONE 10	30° TO 40°

Courtesy United States Department of Agriculture

Chapter 2

Climate Considerations

Climate Considerations for Annuals

Annuals are classified according to their hardiness, that is, the lowest temperature they can safely endure. Hardy annuals will withstand at least mild frosts. Half-hardy plants will tolerate cool weather, but not frost. However, the seeds of half-hardy

ANNUAL CHOICES FOR SPECIAL PLACES

Most annuals are happiest when bathed in sunlight, rooted in average soil, and receiving moderate temperatures. The notable exceptions are:

PLANTS FOR HEAVY SHADE

Begonia, browallia, coleus, fuchsia, impatiens, monkey flower, wishbone flower.

PLANTS FOR PARTIAL SHADE

Ageratum, aster, balsam, black-eyed Susan vine, dianthus, dusty miller, forget-me-not, lobelia, nicotiana, ornamental pepper, pansy, salvia, sweet alyssum, vinca.

PLANTS FOR DRIEST CONDITIONS

African daisy, amaranthus, celosia, dusty miller, gomphrena, kochia, petunia, portulaca, spider flower, statice, strawflower.

PLANTS FOR MOIST AREAS

Aster, balsam, tuberous begonia, black-eyed Susan vine, browallia, calendula, flowering cabbage and kale, forget-me-not, fuchsia, gerbera, impatiens, lobelia, monkey flower, nicotiana, ornamental pepper, pansy, phlox, salpiglossis, stock, wishbone flower.

PLANTS FOR HOTTEST SPOTS

Amaranthus, anchusa, balsam, celosia, coleus, creeping zinnia, Dahlberg daisy, dusty miller, gaillardia, gazania, gloriosa daisy, gomphrena, kochia, triploid marigold, nicotiana, ornamental pepper, petunia, portulaca, salvia, spider flower, statice, strawflower, verbena, vinca, zinnia.

PLANTS FOR COOL CLIMATES

African daisy, tuberous begonia, browallia, calendula, clarkia, dianthus, flowering cabbage and kale, forget-me-not, lobelia, monkey flower, pansy, phlox, salpiglossis, snapdragon, stock, sweet pea, wishbone flower.

plants will withstand frost. Tender annuals, as the name implies, have no tolerance for frost. These plants will do poorly in cool weather. Hardy annuals may be planted in early spring as soon as the ground can be worked. For half-hardy plants, wait until several weeks later to plant. Tender annuals must not be planted until all danger of frost has passed. The table in Chapter 7 provides a useful guide to the hardiness of many popular annuals and indicates the most appropriate temperatures for each one.

In newly planted landscapes, annuals can be used as a "quick cover" while you wait for the shrubs and permanent groundcovers to mature. Depending on the exposure and temperature, a number of good choices are available. For example, in hot climates, choose vinca, portulaca, petunia, or sweet alyssum. In cool areas, select phlox or lobelia.

CLIMATE CONSIDERATIONS FOR PERENNIALS

Foresters, farmers, and gardeners rely heavily on the United States Department of Agriculture's planting zone map for choosing the plants that will grow well in their climate. Updated from time to time, it classifies each region according to its annual minimum temperatures (see map p. 8), and/or the length of its growing season.

The United States and Canada have a wide range of climates, from areas with year-round ice and snow to semitropical regions. Zone 1 is near-tundra, and zones 2 and 3 have extremely low temperatures and short growing seasons. Much of the continental United States falls into zones 4, 5, 6, and 7, where a wide range of plants can be grown. Since zones 9 and 10 have little frost, many semitropical plants can be grown outdoors year-round in these areas.

Gardeners in southern regions face far more problems with heat and drought than their northern neighbors. They frequently need to water daily throughout the summer to keep their gardens thriving, and find it necessary to shade fragile plants during the hottest weather. In some areas, August is a dormant season for plants, and many give up their gardening chores for a few weeks. They return in September to enjoy a long fall season of asters, chrysanthemums, cannas, and similar plants.

Heavy, humus-rich soils are preferable in warm regions because they stay cooler than light, sandy ones. Mulches are extremely valuable, since they help to keep the soil cool and prevent moisture from evaporating rapidly. Trees, hedges, tight fences, and walls can give valuable protection from drying winds and, if carefully positioned, can provide light shade during the heat of the day. You can save time and labor if you choose perennials best suited to your particular southern location. Chapter 9 lists plants that do best in spots that are dry, as well as suggesting ones for particular types of gardens. To select plants wisely, take advantage of your neighbors' experience and observe what is thriving in their gardens.

If you garden in the North, in a mountain climate, or in a cool-weather microclimate that limits the growth of many of your favorite trees and shrubs, it may be an ideal situation for

Certain varieties of the following common perennials are prone to winter loss in subzero climates and protective measures are often necessary. Your northern gardening friends will probably tell you that they have been growing some varieties of these plants for many years without taking winter precautions, however, so don't regard this list as definitive:

Althaea, hollyhock	**Cortaderia,** pampas grass
Anchusa, bugloss	**Gaillardia,** blanket flower
Anemone, Japanese anemone	**Helianthemum,** sunrose
Aubrieta, rockcress	**Kniphofia,** torch lily
Bellis, English daisy	**Lavandula,** lavender
Bergenia	**Penstemon,** beardtongue
Callirhoë, poppy mallow	**Potentilla,** cinquefoil
Ceratostigma, plumbago	**Primula,** primrose
Chrysanthemum	**Salvia,** mealycup sage
Coreopsis, tickseed	

herbaceous perennials. Many such species grow best and bloom over longer periods in areas where summers are cool and evening dews are heavy. Frigid temperatures do not affect them as much as they do woody plants because their tops die down before winter, and snow often mulches the roots.

Some plant varieties imported from warmer climates may suffer, nonetheless, when they are exposed over a long period to low winter temperatures. Since the temperature of the soil rather than the air temperature is the critical factor, a plant may survive when the air temperature falls to -40°F, if there is plenty of snow to serve as insulation, but succumb during a mild winter when there is little snow to prevent the ground from freezing well below the surface.

Consequently, if you garden where the mercury drops below zero and a protective layer of snow is not certain, plant only the hardiest of perennials, unless you are able to cover them with mulch each fall and uncover them at the proper time in the spring. An insulating material such as leaves, straw, or wood chips around the plants helps prevent excessive fluctuations in soil temperature, but the best insurance is to cover the entire perennial garden with a non-matting and nonsmothering material, such as evergreen boughs.

If you are a northern gardener, winter temperatures alone should not govern your choice of plant varieties. Frost is another crucial consideration. Perennials such as anemones, chrysanthemums, gentians, *Hibiscus*, and perennial asters blossom so late in the season that they may flower for only a short time, if at all, where frosts come unusually early.

Chapter 3

COLOR CONSIDERATIONS

COLOR CONSIDERATIONS FOR ANNUALS

Color is probably the most striking aspect of flower bed design. It reflects the personality and mood of your home. Warm tones of yellow, gold, orange, and red attract attention to those sections of the garden where they are used. Blue and violet, on the other hand, create a quieter, more tranquil mood. Warm colors make a planting appear smaller than it actually is, while cool colors make it appear larger.

Keep color schemes simple. Use more than one or two colors only in a bed of the same plant, such as zinnias, impatiens, dahlias, or celosia.

There are a number of possible harmonies you can select. (Refer to the color wheel diagram, below.) Choose *complementary* (opposite) colors such as orange and blue (calendula with lobelia), or violet with yellow (two different varieties of pansies). *Split complementary* color combines one color with the color to either side of its opposite. Examples would be red with blue (salvia and ageratum), or red with yellow (red geraniums with yellow dahlias). Treat pink, a tint of red, the same way as red when designing. Treat violet the same way as purple. *Analogous* color harmony is three colors in a row on the wheel, such as yellow, yellow-orange or gold, and orange (marigolds). *Monochromatic* design is different tones of the same color (pink and/or red geraniums, zinnias, or impatiens).

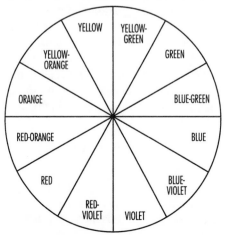

Select one harmony and stay with it throughout the bed or border for best effect.

White blends well with any other color and can also be effective when used alone. Like pastels, especially light pinks, white is most effective when viewed at night, as it reflects moonlight, streetlights, and garden lights. It is best used massed alone or as a unifying border with other annuals. Whites used as buffers between two conflicting colors can often make the design look spotty and disjointed. The same rules that apply to white-flowered annuals apply to white, silver, and gray foliage plants, such as dusty miller.

Color Considerations for Perennials

A bed of annuals is easy to arrange according to color because the same plants stay in bloom all season, but in a perennial border the colors constantly change as different plants come into blossom. It would seem challenging enough to design a perennial garden that appears full of bloom throughout the season, while keeping plants of different heights from obscuring each other. But you should also, ideally, arrange the plants so that their colors remain harmonious, even though the blossoms change from week to week!

It has been said that Mother Nature can throw together flowers of any color and they don't clash as they would in a man-made environment. Yet even in nature colors clash. Gardens that have been planted in thoughtful color combinations have an overall beauty that a hodgepodge can't match. If you have any doubts, take a color photo of both types of borders and compare them.

In a color-coordinated garden the clumps of each color group should not only be of the same variety but also the same shade, rather than a mixture of shades. A dozen pink *Primula* planted together, for example, have a more impressive visual impact than a multicolored clump. The validity of this concept is obvious in parks, where large beds of the same varieties of geraniums, petunias, or marigolds are so effective.

Color in Seasonal Gardens

Seasonal perennial gardens are much easier to design with color in mind, since you do not need a lot of space for great numbers of plants that will blossom throughout the season. Spring tulips, for instance, are especially attractive when grouped in a mass of a single eye-catching color. If you spend only the month of August in a summer home, fill your garden with brightly colored phlox that are separated by clumps of phlox in paler shades or white. It makes a beautiful sight. Other spectacular seasonal gardens can be planted entirely with two or three colors of chrysanthemums or with lilies.

Color Gardens

Another popular concept in gardening design involves the use of a single dominant color throughout. Take as an example a blue and white border enclosed by a low stone wall. Delphinium provides accent points at the corners, and masses of *Polemonium*, campanula, *Cerastium*, iris, Shasta daisy, hosta, *Iberis*, and others bloom at various times throughout the spring, summer, and fall. You can create many other effective beds with a single color such as pink, red, yellow, or blue, combined with white. Some can be planned with the gardener's favorite color in mind, and others with colors that complement their backgrounds — an aging shed of weathered boards, a tall stone foundation where a barn once stood, a sheared evergreen hedge, a wooden fence, or a reflecting pool.

Chapter 4

Landscaping Strategies with Annuals

You are proud of your home. The landscape seems complete. Attractive shrubbery frames the house. Stately trees contribute strength, definition, and shade. Ornamental flowering trees provide attractive accents. The lawn is lush and green, carpeting the complete scene. Yet something is missing.

The only "finishing touch" your home needs may very well be more color. The most rewarding and easiest way to achieve this color is with the use of annual flowers. They create a mood, add another dimension, and enhance the beauty of the home.

Beds or Borders?

The impact that flowers make is a measure of professionalism in the home landscape. Wherever space permits, annual flower beds and/or borders should be included in the overall design. Flower beds are those plantings that are accessible from all sides. An example is an island planting in the middle of the lawn. Borders, on the other hand, are at the edge of an area, be it the lawn, walkway, driveway, foundation, shrub planting, or fence.

Because borders can usually be worked from only one side, do not plant them any deeper than 5 feet at the most, or maintenance will be difficult. Up to that point, they can be as wide as space and looks permit. Beds should be planned in relation to the surrounding area; don't try to situate too large a bed in a small grassed area, or it will be out of proportion.

You can locate beds and borders anywhere on your grounds, uniting plantings of evergreens and flowering trees and shrubs with ribbons of living color.

Special Effects with Annuals

In addition to their primary use in beds and borders, bedding plants can be called upon for a variety of special uses. Flowering vines are unequalled as temporary screens on fences, trellises, or arbors. Select from morning glory, black-eyed Susan vine, cardinal climber, moonflower, sweet pea, scarlet runner bean, or nasturtium.

You may want to bring the beauty of your garden indoors and have cut flowers for the living room. Your flowering annuals can do double duty if you choose types that can be cut and used in arrangements. Frequent cutting of flowers also encourages new growth as well as increased bloom.

Think of annuals as combination plants. While magnificent when used alone, they can also be planted quite effectively with perennials, summer bulbs, and dwarf shrubs. Consider rotating annual plantings over the growing season for the longest-lasting color effect. In warm areas, this can be done year-round. Start with pansies, forget-me-nots, or other cool-temperature plants in spring, followed by any of a large selection of summer annuals, and end the season with another cool favorite such as chrysanthemums or flowering cabbage or kale.

Designing Your Annual World

Design is the next step in creating your colorful world. Decide which plant sizes will best conform to the surroundings. Small beds or edgings along low hedges or beneath foundation plantings demand a low-growing choice, such as ageratum, alyssum, or begonias. In larger areas, you can vary the height to make the effect more interesting, especially if the ground is flat. In a freestanding bed, place taller plants in the center, stepping down to an intermediate-sized plant and then to a ground-hugging annual in front. For a border against a fence or wall, use the tallest in the back and work down to the front.

For a mixed bed or border, choose three sizes of plants. This can be done by combining three varieties of the same plant, such as zinnias or marigolds, that have different heights; or by combining three different plants, such as tall spider flowers and medium-sized dahlias trimmed with a carpet of low-growing petunias.

Plants grow in many different shapes, a mixture of which is most attractive in a mixed bed. Imagine a combination of spiked snapdragons intermingled with mounded begonias and edged with low-growing lobelia. Annuals also grow upright and bushy (African marigolds) or in an open, informal manner (cosmos). Again, try to work in groups of three.

Flowers also come in different shapes, and combining them will make a mixed bed or border more interesting. Examples could be plumes of celosia, gloves of gaillardia, trumpet-shaped petunias, and a wide assortment of single, double, round, daisy-shaped, frilled, or irregularly shaped flowers.

Although combinations are most attractive, they are not a design necessity; a mass planting of one variety of impatiens, for example, in one shape or color, is just as appealing. The decision depends on the effect you want to achieve; a massed planting is sleek and modern in appearance. If the ground is flat, building berms (mounds of soil) for mass plantings will give them height and more perspective.

When you shop for bedding plants or seeds, you will notice that many annuals come in a "series." For example, there are 'Super Elfin Pink,' 'Super Elfin Red,' and 'Super Elfin Blush' impatiens; 'Pink Pearls,' 'Azure Pearl,' and 'White Pearl' petunias; and 'Inca Yellow,' 'Inca Gold,' and 'Inca Orange,' marigolds. If you are planning a massed bed of the same plant in mixed colors, you will achieve greater success if you use plants from the same series. They will be more uniform in height, plant shape, and bloom size.

If space is tight, plant in areas that are most visible. For example, plant annual beds or borders along the walkway or driveway to greet you when you come home, or place them in the backyard where you will be relaxing on weekends.

Shape of the planting area can be influenced by the surroundings. A stately Georgian or very modern house would demand a formal, straight-lined bed. A Colonial home would call for a closely packed, cottage-garden style. Most of today's architecture is complemented by semi-formal, contoured flower beds or borders. Study the dictionary section in Chapter 7 before making a final design decision.

Container Basics

Container growing does require somewhat more maintenance than does caring for the same plants in the ground, but the ability to bring color into the landscape without planting beds makes it worth the effort. The container can be anything that will hold planting media and plants, so long as it has adequate drainage. If the container does not have drainage holes and none can be made, a thick layer of gravel must be placed in the bottom of the planter in order to prevent waterlogging of the roots.

Soil should never be used in container plantings; it is too heavy and can introduce insects and diseases. Mix or purchase a soilless medium of peat moss or bark with perlite and/or vermiculite. Fill the container to about ½ inch from the top before planting, and water well. For a fuller effect, plant closer than you would in the ground.

Containers will need to be watered more than planting beds

will, as the growing area is limited and more apt to dry out. Daily watering may be necessary, so make sure that water is easily accessible. Containers should be fertilized lightly but frequently with a soluble plant food. If light strikes it unevenly, you should rotate the planter to make growth symmetrical.

PLANT SELECTION

Once you've decided to beautify your home with annuals, you must decide which plants to use. There are two considerations: matching the right plant with your growing conditions, and selecting plants for their visual appeal.

Refer to Chapter 7 for lists of plants to be used under a variety of climatic conditions: sun, shade, wet, dry, hot, cool. After you've studied these carefully, consider how much time you can devote to the garden. If your time is limited, choose a low-maintenance plant.

Then decide how much space to allocate to flower beds, estimating your ability to maintain the total space available.

The rest is personal preference. Do you have a color scheme you want to follow? If not, study the section on color to decide what's best for you. Massed beds or mixed borders? Again, that depends on your layout, your style of home, and your personal preference.

Before you do any planting, lay out on graph paper the plan of your garden beds and flowers. This will allow you to decide, in advance, the shape and size of the borders and beds. It will also help you determine how many plants you will need to grow or buy.

Chapter 5

Landscaping Strategies with Perennials

Choosing the Spot

Part of the fun of designing a garden is uniting your chosen plants with a unique location. No other garden in the world will be exactly like yours, because the design of your home, the natural features of the landscape, and the surrounding vistas will make it distinctive. Even if you live in a city and have little or no choice of garden sites, you can still create a garden that has a character all its own.

If your lot is bare — no trees, pool, hedges, or shrubs there already — you will be able to plan a garden with greater freedom. When such things are already installed, you should choose new plantings that will complement what is already there. A perennial bed always looks best if it relates well in size and design to the buildings and other plantings near it.

Certain spots are natural for a flowering border, so look at fences, walls, hedges, walkways, driveways, terraces, buildings, a brook, a pool, specimen trees, or other defined "edges" that could be used as boundaries. Take advantage of whatever you've got.

If all gardens followed the example of formal European borders, it would seem that the only place for a perennial bed is a lawn that is as large and level as a ballroom floor. That kind of area can serve as the setting for a magnificent garden, but most people are neither so ambitious nor so fortunate as to garden under such conditions. As the Japanese have demonstrated so well, gardens can fit nearly any available space. Use your imagination and you may find your grounds are ideal for a colorful flower island, a hillside rock garden, a fern bower in the woods, or a tiny cottage garden planted entirely with old-fashioned colonial plants clustered around the back door.

Since flowering perennials need practically full sun throughout the day, choose a sunny spot if you want a wide range of plants to thrive. Ideally, a perennial garden will continue to grow for years in the same location, so not only make a note of present light conditions, but also try to anticipate what may happen in the future. If you or your close neighbors have young trees growing nearby, the amount of shade will increase as they grow, and some pruning, or perhaps complete removal, of trees will be necessary to ensure adequate sunlight for continued good growth and flowering of your perennials. It is interesting to note as well that certain flowers tend to face the source of light when they are planted in a garden that is shaded for part of the day. Daffodils, most daisy-type flowers, pansies, violas, members of the sunflower family, and spiky flowers such as penstemon all have this habit, so if you plan to grow more than a few of these, position your garden to take best advantage of this tendency.

Good soil is basic to a fine garden, but if the site you choose is not blessed with the best, you can either improve it, or grow only those plants that will tolerate your conditions. For instance, water-loving plants may be planted in wet spots; rock garden or desert-type plants prefer dry, gravelly soil. A more complete discussion on soils and soil improvements can be found in Chapter 8.

Whenever possible, avoid placing plants too close to trees and shrubs, not only because of the shade, but also because their large roots will creep into your beds and rob your plants of nutrients and moisture. It may be difficult to gauge what an adequate distance will be, since the roots of a large shade tree can extend 100 feet or more from the trunk. It is possible to garden near trees, large hedges, and shrubs if the lot gets plenty of sun, and if you provide enough fertilizer and water so that both your garden and the larger plants will be nourished. Some gardeners bury a metal or concrete barrier 2 or more feet deep between a newly planted hedge or shrub border and the garden to keep the roots from venturing where they are not wanted.

If wind is a problem where you live, choose a sheltered spot for your perennials, or create a protected area with hedges or fences. A tall evergreen hedge might serve as a back border, allowing you to grow tall and fragile plants, such as delphinium, hollyhocks, and Oriental poppies, even on a windy hilltop. A basket-weave or picket fence will also offer protection, but unless the confined area is tiny, a tight board fence or one made of fiberglass panels can create powerful downdrafts and cause winds to swirl among the plants, which can inflict as much damage as a direct gale.

Positioning Perennials

The concept of clumping is basic to good garden design. When each plant grows separately and does not touch its neighbor, the garden has an orderly look, and each plant is allowed to reach its full potential. To create the masses of color and the shapes that make perennial borders so attractive, plant clumps of the same variety at intervals throughout the garden. The eye of the observer is drawn from one to the next and a pattern is created. One large peony, Shasta daisy, or lupine clump is often large enough to establish a block or mass of the same color and height; but with smaller plants, such as *Primula* (primrose) and *Heuchera* (coral bells), three, five, or even seven may be used. Odd numbers seem to work best in garden design.

When spacing the plants allow plenty of room for the healthy expansion of each clump, so that it will not impinge on neighboring plants. This takes some discipline, because almost everyone tends to put new small plants too close together. It is difficult to know the amount of space a mature plant will need because each one grows so differently, but as a rule allow at least 1 foot between every plant in a clump, and 2 or more feet between each clump. One vigorous-growing plant, such as a daylily, peony, or gloriosa daisy, may fill an area 3 or 4 feet in diameter within just a couple of years. After a few years of gardening experience, you will be better able to judge how plants grow in your locality, and can decide with confidence how far apart each should be planted.

Even with generous spacing, most perennials will need to be divided from time to time and the clumps reduced to a manageable size. Overgrown gardens not only appear messy and lose their charm, but — even more important — plants that are crowded do not grow or blossom well.

PLANT SIZE

Common sense dictates that plants must be arranged according to height, so that plants such as sweet William and pansies will not be completely hidden behind a tall clump of foxglove. Some gardeners are so impressed by this reasoning that they arrange their borders rigidly according to height: tall plants in the back row, medium-sized ones in the middle, and low-growing ones in front. They plant island gardens the same way, in tiers like a wedding cake, with the tallest plants in the center. But such inflexible arrangements seem almost artificial. A garden is more pleasing to the eye if plants of different heights, colors, and varieties are arranged as if they're growing naturally throughout the garden. An irregular arrangement of heights is made easier and more attractive by the fact that perennials bloom at different times. You can place a Blue

Fountain delphinium near the front of a bed with the confidence that it will have finished blooming and can be cut back before the shorter penstemon behind it starts to flower.

Figuring heights as you design the garden is a tricky business, even for an experienced gardener. Often the different varieties of one species grow to varying heights, and identical varieties may also grow to different sizes, depending on the particular soil, light conditions, and climate. Use plant descriptions only as guides since the plants may behave quite differently given the conditions in your garden.

FLOWERING TIMES

The sequence of bloom is a major factor in the design of a perennial garden, since it is hoped that there will be blossoms throughout the bed from early spring until fall frosts (unless, of

SPRING BLOOMERS

TALL	MEDIUM	SHORT
Columbine	Fernleaf bleeding-heart	Moss pink
Common bleeding-heart	Sweet William	Violet
Leopard's bane	Daylily, early	
Siberian iris	varieties	

EARLY SUMMER BLOOMERS

TALL	MEDIUM	SHORT
Delphinium	Golden Marguerite	English daisy
German iris	Bellflower	Carpathian bellflower
Lupine	Cornflower	Coral bells
Peony	Pyrethrum	
	Daylily	
	Lily	
	Beardtongue	

course, a seasonal garden is planned). Most perennials bloom for only a limited period in their annual life cycle, so both new gardeners and long-time horticulturists complain of "gaps" when the garden produces few, if any, flowers.

Just as it is difficult to estimate the height of perennials, it is also hard to tell exactly when each species will blossom.

Various soils, light conditions, and climate variations can cause identical plants to flower at different times. In addition, identical plants may behave differently from one year to the next. A warm spring may accelerate the blooms, or an unexpected late winter or cool spring is likely to delay the flowering period. In an area with a short growing season, spring often arrives late, and some years the daffodils, *Doronicum, Pulmonaria,* and tulips all bloom at the same time, along with the lilacs and apple trees.

MID- TO LATE SUMMER BLOOMERS

TALL	**MEDIUM**	**SHORT**
Monkshood	Spirea	Crane's bill
Globe thistle	Shasta daisy	Sea lavender
Baby's breath	Blanket flower	Balloon flower
Daylily	Campion	Stokes' aster
Hosta	Tritoma	Betony
Liatris	Coneflower	
Lythrum		
Bee balm		
Phlox		

LATE SUMMER AND FALL BLOOMERS

TALL	**MEDIUM**	**SHORT**
Japanese anemone	Turtlehead	Aster, dwarf varieties
Rose mallow	Chrysanthemum	Chrysanthemum, dwarf
Sage		varieties
		Sedum

Although zone charts are useful as broad guidelines, the expertise of neighboring gardeners will be more precise and valuable. After a season or two of observing perennial plants in your area, you will better understand how they are likely to behave in your garden. Even so, you will probably shuffle plants around for as long as you grow perennials in order to achieve a satisfying design and attractive garden appearance. Keep a notebook handy to record not only blooming times, but also plant heights and combinations that you like. Place plastic tags or signs next to those plants that are to be moved when the time is right.

Chapter 6

Caring for Annuals

Getting Down to Basics — Soil

No matter how well you plan your garden or how high the quality of your plants, you will not succeed without a good foundation: a proper soil. Before planting, you should prepare the soil, especially if a flower bed has never before been in the location where planting will be done. After laying out the area, remove all grass, weeds, stones, and other debris.

Incorporate organic matter such as peat moss, leaf mold, or compost at a rate of about 25 percent of soil volume into the areas where the roots will be growing, which is approximately the top 8 inches. Organic matter will improve moisture retention and drainage. Fertilizer should also be mixed in; choose a kind whose ratio of nitrogen-phosphorus-potassium (N-P-K) is 1:1:1 or 1:2:1, and apply according to label directions. Normal rate of application on new beds is 1 to 2 pounds of 5-10-5, 10-10-10, or similar ratio per 100 square feet. On established beds, a soil test is recommended; normally, 1 pound per 100 square feet would be sufficient. Spade, rototill, or otherwise mix the soil well until it is uniform. Then level it off.

Soil for most annuals should be slightly acid to neutral, with a pH of 5.5 to 7.0. Have your soil's pH tested at your county agricultural extension service, or test it yourself with a soil-test kit.

Beds should not be worked in early spring when the soil is still wet, or the texture will be ruined. Beds can be worked the previous fall, or in spring just before planting.

Planting

If you purchase bedding plants instead of growing your own annuals from seeds, look for deep green, healthy plants that are neither too compact nor too spindly. It is better if they are not yet in bloom. Most annuals will come into full bloom faster in the garden if they are not in bloom when planted.

Most bedding plants are grown in individual "cell packs," although they may be in flats or individual pots. If you can't plant them right away, keep them in a lightly shaded spot and water them as needed. Just before planting, the bedding plants should be well watered, as should the soil in the bed or border.

Do not try to jump the gun at planting time! Refer to the chart on pp. 41-43. Tender annuals cannot be planted until after all danger of frost has passed and the soil is warm. Half-hardy annuals can be safely planted if nights are still cool, as long as there will be no more frost. Hardy and very hardy plants can be planted in early spring as soon as the soil can be worked.

When planting time has come, use the planting distance guide outlined on the chart on pp.41-43. Carefully lift plants from cell packs or pots, keeping the root ball intact in order to avoid damage. The best way to do this is to either gently squeeze or push up the bottom of the container if it is pliable enough, or turn it upside down to have the plant fall into your hand. If the plant does not slide out easily, tap the bottom of the container with a trowel. If the root ball is moist, as it should be, it should slip out easily without being disturbed.

Occasionally, you will find plants in a flat without individual cells. If you do, just before planting separate the plants gently by hand or with a knife so that the roots do not dry out. Other times, plants may be growing in individual peat pots. In this case, either peel most of the pot away, or be sure the top of the pot is below soil level after planting.

If roots are extremely compacted, loosen them gently before planting. Dig a hole slightly larger than the root ball, set the plant in place at the same level at which it was growing, and carefully firm the soil around the roots. Water well soon after planting, and again frequently until plants are established and new growth has started. At that time, an application of soluble fertilizer high in phosphorus will encourage root growth.

To reduce transplanting shock, plant on a cloudy or over-cast late afternoon. Petunias are the most notable exception to this rule, tolerating planting even on hot, sunny days.

Keeping the Garden Colorful

The first steps to a beautiful flower garden, as we have seen, are good soil preparation and proper planting. After that, keeping color at its peak is up to you and Mother Nature. If maintenance is a consideration, choose less demanding annuals. (Refer to the chart on pp.41-43).

Fertilizing

Most annuals do not require high levels of fertilizer, but will do much better if adequate nutrients are available. Notable exceptions are nasturtium, spider flower, portulaca, amaranthus, cosmos, gazania, or salpiglossis, all of which like to be grown in poor, infertile soils. With these, the fertilizer incorporated before planting is adequate. With other annuals, you can fertilize once or twice more during the growing season with 5-10-5 or a similar ratio at the rate of 1 to 2 pounds per 100 square feet. As an alternative, you may use a soluble fertilizer such as 20-20-20, following label directions and applying every 4 to 6 weeks. Over-fertilizing will cause a buildup of soluble salts in the soil, especially if it is heavy soil, and result in damage to the annuals. Over-fertilizing can also result in heavy foliage growth and few flowers.

WATERING

Heavy but infrequent watering encourages deep root growth. Annuals should be watered only as often as the lawn. For guidelines on those plants that like more or less moisture, refer to the individual plant descriptions in the dictionary, or to the chart on pp.41-43. When annuals need less water than the surrounding lawn and shrubbery, or where soil drainage is poor, raised beds are a "must" for uniform and successful growth.

Keep foliage dry during watering. Using soaker hoses is a good way to achieve this. However, if overhead sprinklers must be used, water those annuals that are disease-prone (zinnias, calendula, grandiflora petunias, and stock in particular) as early in the day as possible, so that the foliage will dry out before nightfall, lessening the chance of disease. When you use annuals for cut flowers, avoiding overhead watering will help prevent water damage to the blooms. Where dry soil and dry skies prevail and irrigation is not possible, choose drought-resistant annuals like portulaca, celosia, cosmos, sunflower, amaranthus, candytuft, dusty miller, gazania, spider flower, sweet alyssum, or vinca.

MULCHING

After your annuals are planted, adding a 2- to 3-inch layer of mulch will not only add a note of attractiveness, it will also reduce weeds and conserve soil moisture, resulting in better growth. The best mulches are organic, and include bark chips, pine needles, shredded leaves, peat moss, or hulls of some kind. The following year, the mulch can be incorporated into the soil before planting, thereby enriching it. Additional mulch can be added each spring, resulting in better soil structure and therefore better growth as years pass.

WEEDING

In addition to supplying the basic requirements for good growth, you will want to weed your plants in order to keep beds and borders as appealing as possible. Weeds may appear even if you use mulch and a pre-emergent herbicide. Be sure to remove weeds as soon as possible, so that they do not compete with the flowers for water and nutrients. Remove weeds carefully, especially when the annuals are young, so as not to disturb the annuals' roots.

RESEEDING

Some annuals, notably impatiens, portulaca, salvia, and nicotiana, will reseed from one year to the next. As many annuals are hybrids, the seedlings may not be identical to the parent and will often be less vigorous. It is best to remove these seedlings and replant all flower beds and borders each year for maximum effect. In most areas, the seedlings will never grow large enough to be showy.

MANICURING

Some annuals, chiefly begonias, impatiens, coleus, alyssum, ageratum, lobelia, vinca, and salvia, require little additional care. Their flowers fall cleanly from the plant after fading and do not need to be removed by hand. Others, such as marigolds, geraniums, zinnias, calendula, or dahlias, will need to have faded flowers removed. This is known as deadheading, and it keeps the plants attractive and in full bloom, while preventing them from going to seed or becoming diseased. Deadheading can be performed with pruning shears or sometimes with the fingers.

To be kept compact and freely flowering, a few annuals, primarily petunias, snapdragons, and pansies, may need to be pinched back after planting or after the first flush of bloom. As new hybrids are created, this is becoming less of a maintenance requirement. Sweet alyssum, candytuft, phlox, and lobelia may tend to sprawl and encroach on walks, the lawn, or other flowers. They can be headed back with hedge clippers. This shearing will also encourage heavier blooming.

In the fall, after frost has blackened their tops, annual plants should be removed, so that the beds will not be unsightly through the winter.

Insect and Disease Control

Proper care will help protect annuals from insects and disease. Those annuals mentioned as being prone to diseases should be planted in areas where the air circulation is good, and if possible the foliage should be kept dry. When this cannot be done or when rain is frequent, fungicide treatment may be necessary.

The most common problem insects that might appear are aphids, whitefly, or spider mites; these again are easily controlled with a number of pesticides. Mites and whitefly are less of a problem when moisture levels are high and plants are frequently watered. When temperatures are high, insect populations will increase and more frequent pesticide treatments may be necessary.

Where slugs and snails are common, you will find that they can feast on young annuals, especially marigolds, petunias, and salvia. Place slug bait near new plantings in the late afternoon, and replenish it as necessary. Many of the baits lose their potency after irrigation or rain.

CHAPTER 7

A DICTIONARY OF FLOWERING ANNUALS

AFRICAN DAISY *(Arctotis stoechadifolia)*. Cheerful 3-inch daisies of yellow, white, pink, bronze, red, purple, brown, and orange bloom all summer atop 10- to 12-inch stems. Foliage is white and woolly and is mounded at the base of the plant.
SOIL: Poor, dry.

AGERATUM *(Ageratum Houstonianum)*. Clusters of fluffy, tiny, powderpuff-like flowers of blue, white, or pink bloom all summer on 4- to 8-inch, compact, mounded plants.
SOIL: Rich, average to moist.

AMARANTHUS *(Amaranthus* species*)*. Grown for its bright, flashy, multicolored foliage. Leaves can be red, maroon, chocolate brown, green, yellow, variegated, or splashed with one or more contrasting colors. Also called summer poinsettia.
SOIL: Average, dry, infertile.

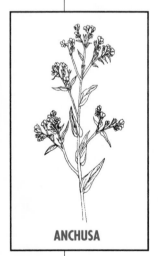

ANCHUSA

ANCHUSA *(Anchusa capensis)*. Clusters of tiny, showy, ultramarine blue flowers on spreading plants 9 to 18 inches tall. Narrow foliage is coarse and hairy. Also called summer forget-me-not or bugloss. Use as a groundcover; in beds or borders.
SOIL: Average to poor.

ASTER *(Callistephus chinensis)*. Single or double blooms of blue, white, lavender, purple, yellow, pink, or red flower atop long cutting stems from midsummer to frost. Flowers have many different forms, including pompon, chrysanthemum, peony, cactus, and plumed.
SOIL: Fertile, rich, moist.

BALSAM *(Impatiens Balsamina)*. This favorite from grandmother's garden has along its stem waxy flowers of white, pink, red, purple, lavender, salmon, or yellow. Long, pointed leaves.
SOIL: Rich, fertile, moist.

BEGONIA, TUBEROUS *(Begonia* x *tuberhybrida)*. Double blooms of red, yellow, orange, white, pink, or combinations of these colors often resemble small roses or camellias.
SOIL: Rich, moist.

BEGONIA, WAX *(Begonia* x *semperflorens cultorum)*. Wax begonias have neat mounds of green or bronze foliage and tiny clusters of pink, white, or red flowers. A good shade plant and one of the easiest annuals to grow. Where heat and humidity are high, use the bronze-leaved varieties. Can be grown in full sun if kept well-watered and temperatures are not over 90°F.
SOIL: Rich, average.

BLACK-EYED SUSAN VINE *(Thunbergia alata)*. A neat, small vine that grows to 6 feet with bell-shaped flowers of white, yellow, or orange, some with black centers. Use as a groundcover, in a hanging basket, or trained on a trellis.
SOIL: Rich, moist.

BROWALLIA *(Browallia speciosa)*. Multitudes of star-shaped, purple, blue, or white flowers bloom all summer long in a shady spot.
SOIL: Rich, moist.

CALENDULA, POT MARIGOLD *(Calendula officinalis)*. Bright 3- to 4-inch blooms of orange or yellow are crisp, single, or double, and daisy- or chrysanthemum-like.
SOIL: Rich, moist.

CANDYTUFT *(Iberis* species*)*. Flowers of white, pink, crimson, rose, carmine, or lavender bloom in upright spikes or domes throughout the summer on mounded plants. If bloom fades, shear the plant back to encourage further flowering.
SOIL: Average to dry.

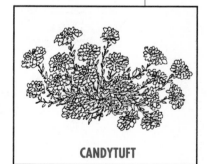

CANDYTUFT

CELOSIA, COCKSCOMB *(Celosia cristata)*. One form of this plant has plumed flowers; the other, crested ones like the comb of a rooster. Flowers are red, rose, pink, yellow, cream, apricot, orange, gold, or salmon. Do not plant too early, as cool weather will cause the plant not to flower at all.
SOIL: Rich, dry.

CLARKIA, GODETIA *(Clarkia* species*)*. Delicate, showy, frilled, single or double flowers — white, pink, salmon, red, lavender, or purple — bloom in spikes along 18- to 24-inch stems.
SOIL: Infertile, average to dry.

COLEUS *(Coleus* x *hybridus)*. Coleus blooms in late summer with tall, thin spikes of blue flowers, but it is grown for its colorful foliage. Leaves have splashy combinations of green, red, chartreuse, white, gold, bronze, scarlet, ivory, orange, salmon, rose, copper, yellow, apricot, pink, or purple!
SOIL: Rich, average to moist.

CORNFLOWER, BACHELOR'S BUTTON *(Centaurea cyanus)*. Double, frilly, ruffled, or tufted flowers of blue (sometimes white or pink) bloom atop wiry stems. Cornflower is not a long-blooming plant, so successive sowings are necessary for continuous color.
SOIL: Average to dry.

COSMOS *(Cosmos* species*)*. *C. bipinnatus* has lacy foliage and daisylike flowers of pink, white, or lavender. *C. sulphureus* has broader leaves and semi-double blooms of flame red, bright yellow, gold, or orange. Use as a border or mass planting.
SOIL: Average to dry, infertile.

CREEPING ZINNIA *(Sanvitalia procumbens)*. Plants hug the ground and spread to 16 inches across, covered with daisylike flowers of yellow or orange with purple centers. Use as a groundcover or in hanging baskets.
SOIL: Average to dry.

DAHLBERG DAISY *(Dyssodia tenuiloba)*. A cheery, fine-textured plant that has simple yellow or orange flowers with yellow centers. Grows only 4 to 8 inches tall.
SOIL: Average to dry.

DAHLIA *(Dahlia* hybrids*)*. Dahlias come in a full range of flower shapes, sizes, and colors (except blue). There are single, double, quill, anemone, cactus, peony, pompon or ball-shaped flowers on dwarf to tall, stately plants. Dahlias can be grown from seeds, plants, or tubers.
SOIL: Rich, moist.

Full-page photo: Cosmos and marigolds. JERRY HOWARD/ POSITIVE IMAGES. **Inset: Globe amaranth (*Amaranthus globosus*).** ROBERT E. LYONS: PHOTO/NATS.

Full-page photo: **Wind flowers (*Anemone blanda*).** MAGGIE OSTER. **Inset: Four-o'clocks (*Mirabilis Jalapa*).** ANN REILLY: PHOTO/NATS.

Full-page photo: Creeping zinnia (*Sanvitalia procumbens*). MAGGIE OSTER. Inset, above: Flowering sage and hibiscus. MADELAINE GRAY. Inset, opposite page: Snapdragons (*Antirrhinum majus*). ANN REILLY: PHOTO/NATS.

Full-page photo: White salvia, spider flowers, and 'Rosy Future' zinnias. MAGGIE OSTER. Inset, below: Peonies. ANN REILLY: PHOTO/NATS. Inset, opposite page: Spider flower (*Cleome Hasslerana*). MADELAINE GRAY.

Full-page photo: Zinnias, sedum, and cosmos in a cottage garden. MARGARET HENSEL/POSITIVE IMAGES. **Inset: *Cosmos bipinnatus.*** ANN REILLY: PHOTO/NATS.

DIANTHUS, CHINA PINK *(Dianthus chinensis)*. These flowers are called pinks, not because they are pink, but because they look as though their petals were cut with a pinking shear. Single or double, frilled, flat-topped flowers of red, white, pink, rose, or lilac are solid-colored or two-toned. Foliage is gray-green and grasslike. Pinks have a clovelike fragrance.
Soil: Rich, alkaline.

DUSTY MILLER *(Chrysanthemum, Centaurea,* or *Senecio* species*)*. Silver or gray leaves are broad in some species, finely cut in others. Use as a buffer between strong colors or as a unifying border. Especially effective in gardens at night, especially if lighted.
Soil: Dry to average.

FLOWERING CABBAGE AND KALE *(Brassica oleracea, Acephala)*. Ornamental cabbage and kale have open rosettes of green leaves with centers of white, pink, or purple. Use as a decorative plant for the fall garden; will stay colorful for several months.
Soil: Rich, moist.

FORGET-ME-NOT *(Myosotis sylvatica)*. For a touch of blue to contrast with spring bulbs, plant forget-me-not seeds the previous fall or set out plants in early spring. Flowers of blue (sometimes pink or white) are tiny but profuse. Use as a groundcover between bulbs, perennials, or on their own.
Soil: Rich, moist.

FOUR O'CLOCK *(Mirabilis Jalapa)*. Lovely, trumpet-shaped, fragrant flowers are white, red, yellow, pink, or violet. Some are solid colors, others are mottled, striped, veined, or splashed with a contrasting color. Flowers open in the afternoon and stay open until the following morning. When skies are cloudy, blooms are open all day.
Soil: Poor.

FUCHSIA *(Fuchsia hybrida)*. Delicate, drooping blooms shaped like a hoop skirt are single or double, in shades of pink, red, white, lavender, blue, orange, yellow, and purple. Flowers are usually two-toned, with long, showy stamens protruding from the center. Use in containers or hanging baskets; in beds or borders in warmer zones.
Soil: Rich, moist.

GAILLARDIA *(Gaillardia pulchella)*. Ball-shaped, double flowers are brilliant red, bronze, butterscotch, or maroon, with fringed petals tipped with yellow. Use in cutting gardens for all-summer bloom.
SOIL: Average to dry.

GAZANIA *(Gazania rigens)*. Single, daisylike blooms atop long stems are yellow, gold, orange, cream, pink, or red with either yellow or dark centers. Use massed in beds or borders; as a groundcover. Flowers close up at night and on cloudy days.
SOIL: Average to dry.

GERANIUM *(Pelargonium* x *hortorum)*. A garden favorite, with round heads of single or double flowers that bloom atop long stems. Flower colors include white, pink, rose, salmon, coral, lavender, and red. Scalloped foliage may be solid green or green with black or brown zoning. Those grown from seed are also more tolerant of high heat and diseases. Cut off flowers as they fade.
SOIL: Rich, moist, fertile.

HIBISCUS

GERBERA, TRANSVAAL DAISY *(Gerbera Jamesonii)*. Gerbera foliage hugs the ground; the plant sends up long stems that are topped with daisylike flowers of orange, red, pink, white, yellow, salmon, or lavender.
SOIL: Rich, moist.

GLORIOSA DAISY *(Rudbeckia hirta)*. Daisylike flowers can be single or double in shades of gold, yellow, bronze, orange, brown, or mahogany. Petals often have dark bands and dark centers. Grow cut flowers; in the wildflower garden; in beds.
SOIL: Rich, average.

GOMPHRENA *(Gomphrena globosa)*. The round, mounded, papery petals of gomphrena appear atop long stems. Flowers are purple, lavender, rose, pink, orange, yellow, and white.
SOIL: Fertile, dry.

HIBISCUS *(Hibiscus* species*)*. If you need a tall, shrubby plant for a screen, hedge, or against a wall, hibiscus is a good choice. Flowers are single, five-petalled, and flare like a trumpet. A

prominent tubular structure protrudes from the center of the flower. Use as screen, hedge, or against a wall.
SOIL: Rich, moist.

IMPATIENS *(Impatiens Wallerana)*. Impatiens are without doubt the most popular flower for the shade. They can be grown in sun, too, if the soil is kept constantly moist, but they will be much larger. Mounded plants are covered all summer with blooms of white, pink, salmon, orange, scarlet, red, and violet. Some blooms have white, starlike centers. Plant under trees; in containers; in a shaded border.
SOIL: Rich, moist, infertile.

IVY GERANIUM *(Pelargonium peltatum)*. Leaves are shaped like ivy, and flowers appear at the ends of long stems. Flowers resemble those of the garden geranium, but are in looser clusters. Blooms may be red, magenta, pink, scarlet, lilac, or white. Use as a groundcover or in hanging baskets.
SOIL: Rich, fertile.

KOCHIA *(Kochia scoparia* forma *trichophylla)*. In fall, this globe-shaped plant turns a bright cherry red and adds color as other annuals are starting to fade. Use as a unique accent or a hedge.
SOIL: Dry, fertile.

LANTANA *(Lantana Camara)*. Lantana is a formal plant that has tiny clusters of flowers that resemble the nonpareil candy. Flowers open in yellow, then change to orange and red, so that all three colors are present at the same time.
SOIL: Rich, fertile.

LAVATERA *(Lavatera trimestris)*. Lavatera has large white, pink, or red flowers that bloom along tall spikes amid maplelike foliage. Use as a background or tall border plant.
SOIL: Average to dry, fertile.

LOBELIA *(Lobelia Erinus)*. Valued for the multitude of tiny, intensely colored flowers that are blue, purple, lavender, or red. Spreads quickly to cover the ground between small shrubs or in the rock garden. If plants become leggy, cut them back to encourage bushiness and heavier bloom. Use as a shade plant, but can be grown in full sun in cool, coastal areas.
SOIL: Rich, moist.

MARIGOLD, AFRICAN *(Tagetes erecta)*. Medium-to-tall, formal plants with large, round, double flowers of yellow, gold, or orange. Use in tall borders, edgings, or as a background plant. Remove flowers as they fade. Be sure African marigolds are in bud or bloom when they are planted; otherwise, they will not bloom until late summer, as they will start to flower only when days become short.
SOIL: Average.

MARIGOLD, FRENCH, TRIPLOID *(Tagetes patula, patula* x *erecta)*. Low-growing, bushy plants with flowers of red, yellow, gold, or mahogany. Flowers may be single, double, crested, or flat. Use as edgings, in borders, beds, or containers. Triploid marigolds do not produce seed, and therefore bloom more heavily. They are also more heat-resistant than other marigolds. Flowers of French marigolds should be removed as they fade.
SOIL: Average.

MEXICAN SUNFLOWER *(Tithonia rotundifolia)*. Most Mexican sunflowers are tall plants with large, daisylike flowers of orange-red or yellow that attract the eye from the far side of the garden. Use as background plants or cut flowers.
SOIL: Dry.

MONKEY FLOWER *(Mimulus* x *hybridus)*. This flower looks like a monkey's face and is yellow, gold, or red, with flecking of a contrasting color. Use in low borders and near water, as it likes moist soil.
SOIL: Rich, moist, fertile.

NASTURTIUM *(Tropaeolum majus)*. Nasturtiums are bushy or vining plants and one of the easiest to grow from seed. Flowers are funnel-shaped and red, yellow, or orange. Leaves are dull and round. Use dwarf varieties in beds and borders; climbing varieties on trellises or supports. Nasturtium flowers, leaves, and buds are all edible and can be used in salads.
SOIL: Dry, infertile.

NEW GUINEA IMPATIENS *(Impatiens* 'New Guinea')*. This relatively new discovery in the plant world has flowers that resemble the garden impatiens in shades of lavender, orange, red, pink, salmon, and purple. It is, however, grown for its colorfully marked foliage of green, yellow, and cream. Use in beds, borders, hanging baskets, and containers. Containers may be

brought indoors in winter and grown in high light.
SOIL: Rich, moist.

NICOTIANA, FLOWERING TOBACCO *(Nicotiana alata)*. Grandmother grew the nicotiana, but today's hybrids are different from her plants. They are compact, shorter, and unfortunately without most of the fragrance they used to have. Trumpet-shaped flowers of yellow, purple, green, red, pink, or white bloom in loose clusters all summer. It prefers high humidity.
SOIL: Rich, moist.

ORNAMENTAL PEPPER *(Capsicum annuum)*. Small plants are covered with round, cone-shaped, or tapered peppers that change in color from cream to purple to red. Use in low borders, edgings, or containers.
SOIL: Rich, moist.

PANSY *(Viola* x *Wittrockiana)*. The happy faces of pansies are a welcome sight in any spring garden. Flowers of red, white, blue, pink, bronze, yellow, purple, lavender, or orange are solid-colored or two-toned. Many have a dark blotch that gives the flower the look of a face. Use in beds, borders, or containers. In warm areas, they may be planted in fall and will live over the winter for early spring bloom. In hot areas, hybrids will be more heat-resistant and will last longer into the summer.
SOIL: Rich, moist, fertile.

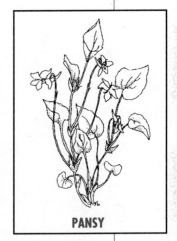

PANSY

PETUNIA *(Petunia* x *hybrida)*. Popular for over a century, petunias have single or double, trumpet-shaped flowers that bloom on spreading plants. Blooms are in every color, some solid, others splashed, starred, zoned, speckled, striped, veined, or margined with a contrasting color. Many have frilled petals. Use grandifloras (large flowers) for containers; multifloras (a profusion of small flowers) for mass plantings. Multifloras are more weather- and disease-tolerant than grandifloras. If plants become leggy, cut them back and they will quickly rebloom.
SOIL: Dry, sandy.

PHLOX *(Phlox Drummondii)*. Low, compact, mounded plants are covered with clusters of round or star-shaped flowers.

37

Colors include white, pink, blue, red, salmon, and lavender. Plant in edgings, borders, or rock gardens. Shear plants after their first bloom to encourage a second, heavy flowering.
SOIL: Fertile, rich, moist.

PORTULACA, MOSS ROSE *(Portulaca grandiflora)*. Flowers are ruffled and pink, red, gold, yellow, cream, orange, white, or salmon. Single blooms are cup-shaped; double flowers resemble tiny roses. Use in hot, dry areas, as a groundcover.
SOIL: Dry, infertile.

SALPIGLOSSIS, PAINTED TONGUE *(Salpiglossis sinuata)*. Tubular, velvety, trumpet-shaped flowers of purple, red, yellow, blue, or rose are heavily veined or textured. Use as an excellent substitute for petunias in areas where summers are cool and moist and petunias won't do well.

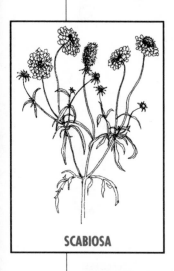

SCABIOSA

SALVIA *(Salvia splendens)*. Salvia is best-known for the red-flowering varieties, but there are plants available with white, coral, or purple-blue flowers. Spikes of blooms appear above the dark green leaves throughout the summer.
SOIL: Rich, average to moist.

SCABIOSA, PINCUSHION FLOWER *(Scabiosa atro-purpurea)*. The blooms of the pincushion flower look exactly like its name. Dark, silvery gray filaments extend from the centers of blue, pink, purple, rose, white, or red double, fragrant flowers.
SOIL: Rich, alkaline, moist.

SNAPDRAGON *(Antirrhinum majus)*. The original snapdragons resembled the jaws of a dragon ready to snap. Today, there are also open-faced and double flowers. Showy, erect spikes have flowers of red, bronze, pink, white, rose, yellow, scarlet, primrose, apricot, orange, crimson, magenta, or lilac and have a light, spicy fragrance. Pinch them back after planting to encourage bushiness and more flowers.
SOIL: Rich, fertile.

SPIDER FLOWER *(Cleome Hasslerana)*. The spider flower has large flowers with very long stamens that look like spiders' legs.

Fragrant flowers are white, rose, pink, or lavender. This is a tall, graceful plant that needs no staking.
SOIL: Dry.

STATICE *(Limonium sinuatum)*. One of the best everlastings is the delicate, light, airy, paperlike flower of the statice. Tiny flowers form in clusters and are purple, blue, yellow, red, or white. Stems are long and stiff.
SOIL: Sandy, dry.

STOCK *(Matthiola incana)*. Stock has stiff spikes of cross-shaped, single, or double flowers of red, white, cream, pink, rose, blue, or purple. It is one of the best flowers for fragrance.
SOIL: Rich, moist, fertile.

STRAWFLOWER *(Helichrysum bracteatum)*. Stiff, brightly colored, papery flowers are red, salmon, purple, yellow, pink, or white. Stems are thin and wiry. Excellent for drying.
SOIL: Dry, fertile.

SUNFLOWER *(Helianthus annuus)*. Sunflowers have long been known as coarse, tall plants used for screening and to attract birds, but there are dwarf varieties available. Daisylike blooms are yellow, bronze, gold, brown, mahogany, cream, or crimson, with dark centers. Use for garden borders and low hedges.
SOIL: Dry, infertile.

SUNFLOWER

SWEET ALYSSUM *(Lobularia maritima)*. Domed clusters of tiny, sweetly scented flowers of white, rose, lavender, or purple cover low-growing plants. Foliage is small and needlelike. Plant in raised planters, or as a low border or edging, where its fragrance can be enjoyed.
SOIL: Average to moist.

SWEET PEA *(Lathyrus odoratus)*. A long-time garden favorite for its delicious fragrance, sweet pea is a vining or bushy plant with blooms of purple, rose, red, white, pink, or blue. Some are solid colors; others are two-toned. Use to cover trellises from early spring until the weather turns hot (vining types); as borders or low hedges (bushy types).
SOIL: Rich, alkaline, fertile, moist.

VERBENA *(Verbena x hybrida)*. For bright coloration in a garden bed, it's hard to beat verbena. Flowers are red, white, violet, purple, blue, cream, rose, or pink, appearing in clusters of tiny flowers. Use in a rock garden or hanging basket.
SOIL: Poor, dry to average.

VINCA, PERIWINKLE *(Catharanthus roseus)*. Leathery, green leaves are topped with five-petalled flowers of rose or white on spreading or upright plants. Some of the flowers have a red center. Vinca is one of the best annuals to plant where air pollution is a problem. Use as a border or edging plant; as a groundcover.
SOIL: Any.

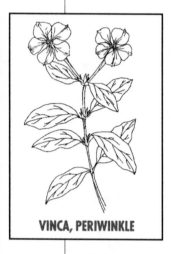

VINCA, PERIWINKLE

WISHBONE FLOWER *(Torenia Fournieri)*. Although the flowers of the wishbone flower are small, there are so many of them that you can barely see the foliage. In the throat of the flower is a pair of stamens that looks like a wishbone. The flowers have a light violet upper lip, a dark purple lower lip, and a yellow throat.
SOIL: Moist, rich.

ZINNIA *(Zinnia elegans)*. It's a shame that one of the best garden flowers is always last on the list. Zinnias are a diverse group of annuals, from the dwarfest to the tallest, in all colors except true blue, and in many flower shapes and forms. Zinnia's main drawback is its disposition to mildew, so plant it where air circulation is good, and water it only in the morning.
SOIL: Average to dry.

ANNUAL SELECTION CHART

	Planting Distance	Maintenance	Plant Height	Light	Moisture	Temperature	Hardiness
African daisy	8-10"	medium	10-12"	S	d	c	H
Ageratum	5-7"	low	4-8"	S, PSh	a-m	m	HH
Amaranthus	15-18"	medium	18-36"	S	d	m-h	HH
Anchusa	8-10"	medium	9-18"	S	d-a	m-h	HH
Aster	6-18"	high	6-30"	S, PSh	m	m	HH
Balsam	10-15"	low	12-36"	S, PSh	m	h	T
Begonia, tuberous	8-10"	low	8-10"	PSh, Sh	m	c-m	T
Begonia, wax	7-9"	low	6-8"	S, PSh, Sh	a	m	HH
Black-eyed Susan vine	12-15"	medium	3-6"	S, PSh	m	m	HH
Browallia	8-10"	low	10-15"	PSh, Sh	m	c	HH
Calendula	8-10"	high	3-4"	S, LSh	m	c-m	H
Candytuft	7-9"	low	8-10"	S	d-a	any	HH
Celosia	6-8"	low	6-15"	S	d	m-h	HH
Clarkia	8-10"	high	18-24"	S, LSh	d-a	c	H
Coleus	8-10"	low	10-24"	PSh, Sh	a-m	m-h	T
Cornflower	6-12"	medium	12-36"	S	d-a	m	VH
Cosmos	9-18"	medium	18-30"	S	d-a	m	HH
Creeping zinnia	5-7"	medium	5-16"	S	d-a	m-h	HH
Dahlberg daisy	4-6"	low	4-8"	S	d-a	m-h	HH
Dahlia	8-10"	high	8-15"	S, LSh	a-m	m	T

LIGHT:
S = Full sun
LSh = Light shade
PSh = Part shade
Sh = Full Shade

MOISTURE:
d = dry
a = average
m = moist

TEMPERATURE:
c = cool (below 70° F.)
m = moderate
h = hot (above 85° F.)

HARDINESS:
VH = very hardy, will withstand heavy frost
H = hardy, will withstand light frost
HH = half hardy, will withstand cool weather, but not frost
T = tender, will do poorly in cool weather, will not withstand frost

	Planting Distance	Maintenance	Plant Height	Light	Moisture	Temperature	Hardiness
Dianthus	7-9"	low	6-10"	S, PSh	a	c-m	HH
Dusty miller	6-8"	low	8-10"	S, PSh	d-a	m-h	HH
Flowering cabbage, kale	15-18"	low	15-18"	S	m	c	VH
Forget-me-not	8-12"	low	6-12"	PSh	m	c	H
Four o'clock	12-18"	low	18-36"	S	d-a	any	T
Fuchsia	8-10"	high	12-24"	PSh, Sh	m	m	T
Gaillardia	8-15"	medium	10-18"	S, LSh	d-a	m-h	HH
Gazania	8-10"	high	6-10"	S	d-a	m-h	HH
Geranium	10-12"	high	10-15"	S	a-m	m	T
Gerbera	12-15"	medium	12-18"	S	m	m	HH
Gloriosa daisy	12-24"	low	18-36"	S, LSh	a	m-h	HH
Gomphrena	10-15"	medium	9-30"	S	d	m-h	HH
Hibiscus	24-30"	medium	48-60"	S, LSh	m	m	H
Impatiens	8-10"	low	6-18"	PSh, Sh	m	m	T
Ivy geranium	10-12"	medium	24-36"	S	a	m	T
Kochia	18-24"	low	24-36"	S	d	m-h	HH
Lantana	8-10"	medium	10-12"	S	a	m	T
Lavatera	12-15"	medium	18-30"	S	d-a	m	H
Lobelia	8-10"	low	3-5"	S, PSh	m	c-m	HH
Marigold, African	12-15"	high	18-30"	S	a	m	HH
Marigold, French	3-6"	high	5-10"	S	a	m	HH
Mexican sunflower	24-30"	medium	48-60"	S	d	m-h	T
Monkey flower	5-7"	low	6-8"	PSh, Sh	m	c	HH
Nasturtium	8-12"	low	12-24"	S, LSh	d	c-m	T
New Guinea impatiens	10-12"	low	10-12"	S, LSh	m	m	T

	Planting Distance	Maintenance	Plant Height	Light	Moisture	Temperature	Hardiness
Nicotiana	8-10"	low	12-15"	S, PSh	m	m-h	HH
Ornamental pepper	5-7"	low	4-8"	S, PSh	m	m-h	HH
Pansy	6-8"	medium	4-8"	S, PSh	m	c	VH
Petunia	10-12"	medium	6-12"	S	d	m-h	HH
Phlox	7-9"	low	6-10"	S	m	c-m	H
Portulaca	6-8"	low	4-6"	S	d	h	T
Salpiglossis	10-12"	medium	18-24"	S	m	c	HH
Salvia	6-8"	low	12-24"	S, PSh	a-m	m-h	HH
Scabiosa	8-12"	high	12-24"	S	m	m	HH
Snapdragon	6-8"	medium	6-15"	S	a	c-m	VH
Spider flower	12-15"	low	30-48"	S	d	m-h	HH
Statice	12-24"	medium	12-36"	S	d	m-h	HH
Stock	10-12"	high	12-24"	S	m	c	H
Strawflower	7-9"	medium	15-24"	S	d	m-h	HH
Sunflower (dwarf)	12-24"	high	15-48"	S	d	h	T
Sweet alyssum	10-12"	low	3-5"	S, PSh	a-m	m	H
Sweet pea	6-15"	medium	24-60"	S	m	c-m	H
Verbena	5-7"	medium	6-8"	S	d-a	h	T
Wishbone flower	6-8"	low	8-12"	PSh, Sh	m	c	HH
Vinca	6-8"	low	4-12"	S, PSh	any	m-h	HH
Zinnia	4-24"	high	4-36"	S	d-a	m-h	T

Light:
S = Full sun
LSh = Light shade
PSh = Part shade
Sh = Full Shade

Moisture:
d = dry
a = average
m = moist

Temperature:
c = cool (below 70° F.)
m = moderate
h = hot (above 85° F.)

Hardiness:
VH = very hardy, will withstand heavy frost
H = hardy, will withstand light frost
HH = half hardy, will withstand cool weather, but not frost
T = tender, will do poorly in cool weather, will not withstand frost

CHAPTER 8

CARING FOR PERENNIALS

SELECTING THE RIGHT PLANTS

It may be tempting to choose perennial species for your garden by looks alone. But, as in choosing a spouse, you need to be aware of what is unseen before you take the plunge. The thousands of different perennial garden species vary widely in their growing and blooming habits, and each has different needs that must be met in order to thrive.

Garden catalogs, with their stunning photos, can be fun and inspirational to read, but with the exception of a few, they are not the best sources for growing information. Extraordinary varieties may be touted which, in fact, have only modest blooms, are weak, short-lived, and demand a great deal of attention. It takes a strong will to resist reaching for your checkbook when the catalogs arrive in the middle of winter, but try to hold off until you are familiar with the varieties. Either read about the plants you'd like to grow, find out if other local gardeners have had success with them, or try to see them in bloom at a nursery or in a neighbor's garden before allotting them space in your own backyard.

LIGHT AND SOIL PREFERENCES

Although certain plants prefer to grow in partial shade, most common perennials do best in full sunlight. Many, however, can get by beautifully if they receive only a half day of full sun and are exposed to skylight for the remainder of the day. Skylight can be defined as light from an "open" sky, with shading provided by a vertical surface such as a wall, hedge, or building, rather than the canopy of a tree.

The amount of light a perennial needs for good growth and flowering can also be affected by the latitude in which it is found. A variety that needs a location with full sun in the North may do well in a spot with much less light in southern climates because the intensity of light is greater there. Likewise, a plant that prefers partial shade in the South may not need such protection in a northern valley where there are many overcast days. And, in northern latitudes, gardeners may find that plants growing in full sun in June are shaded by trees or buildings in August when the angle of the sun's path is nearer the horizon.

Light exposure affects plants in other ways, too. Many, like peonies, bloom later in the season when grown on the west side of a building than they would in a sunny southeastern exposure. Plants such as chrysanthemums bloom earlier if they are grown where they get early afternoon shade because their blossoming mechanism is triggered by diminishing light conditions. And the blossoms of some plants are more beautiful when they are grown in shaded conditions. The *Hemerocallis* genus as a whole blooms best in full sunlight, but the blossoms of certain red and pink varieties are brighter when the plants are partially shaded from the bleaching effects of hot afternoon sun.

Most common perennials grow best when planted in the same type of soil you would prepare for a vegetable garden. There are, however, plants that prefer dry soil, others that like it moist, and some which grow only in water. Most thrive when the soil has a pH of 5.5 to 6.5, but again there are exceptions. Wild orchids need conditions that would be far too acidic for most plants, and delphinium does best in a more alkaline soil.

The description of each perennial in Chapter 9 lists any special light and soil requirements it may have.

PREPARING THE BED

Although a garden can be started from scratch in the spring, the ideal time to prepare a new bed is in early fall. By tilling it deeply then and again in the spring you can eliminate most of the weeds before planting.

A small plot can be spaded up by hand, but for a large one you'll need to use a garden tractor or rototiller to break up the soil. Avoid using a large farm tractor, either to till or spread fertilizer, because heavy machinery compacts the soil nearly as much as a tiller loosens it. Since the root systems of many perennials grow deep, work the soil to a depth of at least 2 feet. Remove all weed roots and rocks at this time because it will be much more difficult, if not impossible, to get rid of them after the garden has been planted.

Tilling in topsoil is the fastest way to remedy a bad soil condition, but obtaining good topsoil is difficult in many areas and it may be very expensive. Fortunately there are other methods: One is to till the site thoroughly in the fall and sow a cover crop of winter rye. The thickly planted grain stalks not only choke out weeds, but add humus to the soil when it is tilled under in the spring. An alternative is to plant rye, buckwheat, oats, or millet in the spring, and till it under in the fall. A second tilling the following spring thoroughly pulverizes the soil and breaks down all the green material.

If your soil appears to be in good shape it may only need enriching with compost or manure. Simply apply the manure or compost after the first tilling, and till or spade it thoroughly until the sod is broken into fine particles and the humus is well mixed into the soil.

If your plot is not large, and you have time and a strong back, the old-fashioned "double dig" method is the best way to prepare the soil for a long-lasting perennial bed. With a spade, at one end of the garden plot, dig a trench about 2 feet wide along the width of the bed, to a depth of 1 foot. Place the sod and soil on a sheet of plastic. Add to the hole a mixture of compost-manure or plain compost, and thoroughly mix this with the soil

HOW TO IMPROVE YOUR SOIL

CLAY. Lighten heavy clay or clay-loam soil by tilling in sand. A large amount may be necessary if your soil is extremely heavy, and additional sand may be needed every few years as it gradually disappears into the subsoil. Humus is likely to be lacking in such soils. Add manure, peat moss, or compost, if necessary. It may also be helpful to grow a cover crop such as oats or rye for a season and till it into the soil before planting.

GRAVEL OR SANDY. Dry, light soil needs compost, manure, or peat moss in greater than normal amounts. Till in one or more cover crops, too. If you don't want to take the time to improve the soil in this way, or if it is in particularly bad condition, spread rich topsoil on the spot 6 to 12 inches deep and till it thoroughly.

SWAMPY WET. If there is low ground nearby, consider draining the area with ditches or drain tile, then add sandy topsoil to raise the low-lying beds a foot or more. The easiest option, of course, is to leave the area as it is and grow some of the interesting plants that thrive in water or damp spots.

Since heavy sod is difficult to spade or till you can save work by first covering the site with clear plastic to kill off any existing plant life. The sun will bake the plants under the plastic, as well as germinate and kill most of the dormant seeds, all within a few weeks.

at the bottom to a depth of another foot. Then dig up the next 2-foot width. Place the sod from the second hole upside down into the first hole and spread over it a balanced dry organic or chemical fertilizer. Use 3 pounds for each 100 square feet of garden, or the equivalent of a 5-foot by 20-foot plot. Cover it with the remaining soil. Continue in the same manner throughout the garden and in the final hole place the sod and soil you have saved from the first dig.

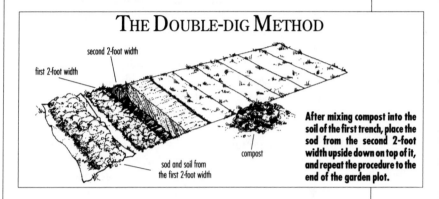

THE DOUBLE-DIG METHOD

second 2-foot width

first 2-foot width

sod and soil from
the first 2-foot width

compost

After mixing compost into the soil of the first trench, place the sod from the second 2-foot width upside down on top of it, and repeat the procedure to the end of the garden plot.

NUTRIENTS

Whether you garden organically or rely on chemicals will determine which steps you take to improve the soil's fertility. Well-rotted farm manure and compost not only add humus, but like other organic fertilizers — kelp, fish emulsion, dried manure, and bonemeal — also supply nutrients. Manure often carries weed seeds, though, so it's best to let it sit for a year before adding it to the soil. Organic fertilizers are less likely than chemical fertilizers to "burn" the plants if you give them an overdose, but unless you have a good supply nearby, or gather your own materials, organic plant food is apt to cost more than the chemical kind. In addition, the nutrient value of organic products can vary widely.

Chemical fertilizers contain nutrients that are absorbed by most plants in sufficient quantities, but many of them are so soluble that they leach away quickly in the soil. Therefore, subsequent applications throughout the season may be necessary. Determining the correct amount is tricky: when too much is applied the rapid availability of chemicals can cause the fertilizer to "burn" a plant (browning of the leaves), which stunts growth and often kills the plant outright. The stimulation of too much rapid growth can also produce weak, unhealthy plants that are susceptible to insects and diseases. In an attempt to overcome the problems of leaching and plant burn, manufacturers have developed a variety of slow-release fertilizers that safely provide food for the plants all summer long with only one

47

application in early spring. When using chemicals of any kind, be sure to follow the directions exactly and remember that more is almost never better.

Organic gardeners use manure and compost as basic soil conditioners. They supply humus and nutrients to the soil as well, but additional fertilizer is often necessary for successful plant growth. Many organic fertilizers, such as cottonseed meal, bloodmeal, and tankage (animal wastes from butcher shops), are used to supply nitrogen and other nutrients. Greensand, wood ashes, and granite dust provide potash; bonemeal and rock phosphate furnish phosphorus. Seaweed and fish oils are rich in the most necessary nutrients and also provide trace elements such as boron, manganese, and others that are necessary in minute amounts for good growth, but are occasionally lacking in worn-out soils. You can have a sample of your soil tested by your county agricultural extension service to see if it is deficient in these trace minerals. If you use manure or composted leaves, the small amount of trace minerals necessary should already be available to the plants.

If you use commercially dried cow or sheep manure, spread at least 10 pounds over each 100-square-foot plot (10 feet by 10 feet) before the final tilling. Farm manure in its natural state can be used safely in varying amounts, but since it has a much higher moisture content than dried manure, 100 pounds per 100 square feet is the recommended ratio. Poultry manure is richer, but it can "burn" plants and should be applied at only one-third of the above rate.

To prepare the soil in an existing garden to which you are adding new perennials (rather than establishing an entire garden bed), dig a large hole deep enough for each plant and add a shovelful of farm manure (or a cup of dried manure) to the bottom. Cover it with a thin layer of soil and then plant the perennial. Water thoroughly and fill in the rest of the hole with rich topsoil or compost.

Edgings

Just as important as the preparation of soil is the establishment of proper garden edgings. They are needed to protect the perennial bed from weeds which can invade the garden either by dropping seeds lifted in by the wind, or by sneaking their roots in subversively from the sides. Although airborne weed seeds are nearly impossible to keep out, edgings are a good way to check the growth of the root-penetrating kind. An edging serves other worthwhile purposes as well. It defines exactly

Full-page photo: Marigolds, geraniums, and ageratum. JERRY HOWARD/POSITIVE IMAGES. **Inset:** 'Universal Blue' pansies (*Viola* x *Wittrockiana*). MAGGIE OSTER.

Full-page photo: Perennial garden with lavender, balloon flowers, tickseed, and *Liatris*. MAGGIE OSTER. Inset, above: Rose campion (*Lychnis coronaria*). MAGGIE OSTER. Inset, opposite page: Coral bells (*Heuchera sanguinaria*). GAY BUMGARNER: PHOTO/NATS.

Full-page photo: China pinks (*Dianthus chinensis*).
ANN REILLY: PHOTO/NATS. **Inset: Pink poppies.**
MAGGIE OSTER.

Full-page photo: **Yellow celosia.** MAGGIE OSTER. **Inset, above:** *Iris reticulata.* MAGGIE OSTER. **Inset, opposite page: Wishbone flower (*Torenia Fournieri*).** ANN REILLY: PHOTO/NATS.

Full-page photo: A yellow and white mixed border with astilbe, baby's breath, and dahlias. MAGGIE OSTER. **Inset: Balloon flower (*Platycodon grandiflorus Mariesii*).** ANN REILLY: PHOTO/NATS.

what is garden and what is not, and gives a bed a finished appearance, often making the difference between a fine garden and a mediocre one.

Install an edging when you first prepare the bed. If you want a straight-edged border, use a taut string tied to stakes at each end as a guide. An irregular or curved bed can be created by using a rope, clothesline, or garden hose in a similar way.

In many gardens the edging is simply a narrow strip of bare earth about 8 inches wide between the flowers and lawn. These were once very popular and the edging tool used to create them—a sharp blade on a straight handle—was an indispensable piece of equipment for the serious gardener. Such a cut-out edging is attractive, but because it must be recut frequently it is less used today.

Plastic, steel, or aluminum edgings take longer to install initially, but they make effective, long-lasting barriers. They are available at most hardware and garden stores, and can be bent easily to fit beds of any shape, which makes them useful for an island garden or a pathway, as well as for a straight border.

The depth of edging you need depends on the type of growth that surrounds your garden. A 4-inch depth will keep out shallow-rooted weeds and most lawn grasses, but 8 inches will do the job even better. Edgings that are 2 or more feet in depth are necessary to halt the deep-roving roots of shrubs and hedges. To install one — after marking the edge of the border — dig a ditch straight down to the necessary depth. Sink the edging vertically, but make sure the top edge is level with the soil so it won't be visible or interfere with mowing the lawn.

PLANTING

After the bed is prepared and the edging in place you're ready for the fun — planting the perennials.

You want to keep the soil loose to allow plant roots to grow easily, so try to compact it as little as possible when working in the garden, both at planting time and later. Don't walk on the soil unless necessary, especially when it is wet. You can reach into a narrow bed from the outside, but in a wide one you may want to lay down boards to absorb the pressure of your weight. There is rarely any reason to do all your planting the same day; rather, do it in stages as you acquire new plants. Most newly planted borders look sparse, but if you want a full bed the first season stick in annual bedding plants as fillers.

Because potted perennials can be planted successfully

throughout the season, it's best to buy the varieties you want in containers: they suffer no transplant shock because every root stays intact. Mail-order plants that are shipped bare-rooted, and other bare-rooted perennials, are best planted during spring in northern zones so they will have time to become well established before winter. South of Zone 5, either fall or spring planting is equally good.

Plants that are freshly dug from a nursery or a friend's garden can be moved easily in the spring, although most perennials can be transplanted all summer if they are handled carefully. Those that go into a short, partly dormant period directly after blooming — bearded iris, bleeding-heart, peonies, Madonna lilies, *Doronicum,* and Oriental poppies, for instance — are best moved at that time. Fall is the ideal time for planting lilies and the early-blooming spring bulbs.

Bare-Rooted Plants

When a bare-rooted plant arrives from a mail-order nursery the roots are usually covered with sphagnum moss or other moisture-retaining material. Unpack the plant immediately and, if it looks dry, soak it in a pail of water for a few minutes. Then plant it according to the enclosed directions. If you must wait a few days before planting, store the plant in a cool, dark place in the packing material, but never leave it soaking in water for long periods.

Evenings or cloudy days are the best times to plant bare-rooted stock because it won't dry out quickly. Treat plants that are out of soil like fish out of water. Always keep the roots covered with moist burlap or a wet towel to avoid the drying

Set a bare-rooted perennial into the soil according to how the roots grow, and then fill in.

effects of sun or wind. Careless treatment of bare-rooted plants is responsible for more unnecessary casualties than all other poor planting techniques combined!

When examining your new bare-rooted perennial, you'll notice that the roots extend from the top part known as the crown. Set the plant into the soil by positioning its roots according to their apparent growth habit, either by spreading them outward or downward. Most perennials should be set at the same depth at which they were previously growing. It is easy to find this level if the old soil line is visible on the stem (or stems). If you aren't sure about the proper depth, arrange the plant so that the top of the root area — the bottom of the crown — is an inch below the soil. Notable exceptions to this rule are peonies and bearded iris. Set peonies so that the base of the red sprout on the uppermost part of the root is *not more* than three-quarters of an inch to an inch below the soil's surface. If it is deeper, the plant will not produce flowers for many years. Since iris roots, too, must be barely covered for best results, set the crown at ground level.

The best planting method is to dig a hole that is twice as large as the root ball with a spade or trowel; never try to squeeze the roots into a small hole. Mix a small amount of compost and a few tablespoons of manure with the soil you removed from the hole, and half fill the hole with water. This old-time practice — called "puddling" — ensures

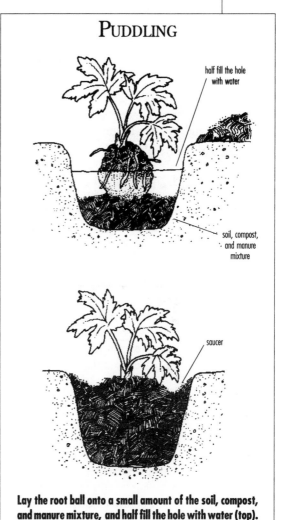

PUDDLING

half fill the hole with water

soil, compost, and manure mixture

saucer

Lay the root ball onto a small amount of the soil, compost, and manure mixture, and half fill the hole with water (top). Fill the rest of the hole, but leave a saucer around the plant (bottom).

that crucial moisture will reach the bottom of the roots. Put a little of the soil you have prepared into the hole and set the plant into it. Finish filling the hole with the soil mix. The muddy mixture will force out any air pockets that might dry out the roots. Firm the soil carefully, but leave a slight depression, or saucer, around each plant to catch the rain and future waterings.

Not everyone uses the puddle method, preferring to simply set the plant in loosened soil and water it well. Whichever method you choose, create a saucer around each plant to ensure that water will reach the roots, and tamp the soil firmly by stepping on it to ensure there will be no air pockets.

POTTED PLANTS

If the soil in the pot is dry, water it thoroughly so that the plant roots will be completely soaked. Dig a hole somewhat larger and deeper than the pot size to accommodate a compost and soil mix around the root ball that will encourage new root growth. Then proceed to plant.

Usually the plant will pop out of its container easily if you turn it over and tap it gently on the bottom, but if it sticks insert a knife around the edge, just as if you were removing a cake from its tin. Keep the root ball intact and set it in the hole so the top of the root ball is just beneath the surface of the soil.

WATERING

Water both bare-rooted and potted plants immediately after planting. Add a bit of liquid seaweed, fish emulsion, manure, or liquid chemical fertilizer with the water to get the plant off to a fast start. After the initial watering, continue to water every day thereafter for a week or two, unless it rains hard. Once the plants are well established, water them only when the soil is dry.

BULBS

Most bulbs need to be in a cultivated, weed-free bed if they are to thrive. Spring-blooming bulbs should be planted in early fall so they will have a chance to develop roots before the ground freezes, but lilies and summer-blooming bulbs can be planted in either spring or fall. Use a trowel, dibble, or bulb planter, and set them, pointed side up, at the appropriate depth. Keep in mind that, even though bulbs bloom and remain green for only a short time, they need regular fertilizing, dividing, and care like other perennials.

If you have a weed, disease, or insect problem that you can't control by recommended "natural" methods, check with your local garden center to find the safest treatments available. If you do spray or dust with pesticides, "spot" spray as much as possible, apply them exactly as recommended on the label, use only as much as is necessary, and store them in a secure place. Be sure to protect yourself: wear gloves, a hood, long pants, and a long-sleeved shirt (old clothes to which you have no attachment). Gardeners with small children should be especially careful when using and storing pesticides and herbicides, just as you would with drugs and medicines.

Pesticides are sold in powder and liquid form. The powders can be applied with a hand duster, mixed with water and sprayed, or sprinkled on with an old watering can (that won't then be used on vegetables). Never spray chemicals on plants that are in bloom, because bees may take the poisons back to their hive. The "flit gun," or hand-held sprayer, is an excellent tool for pest control in a small garden because it is easily directed and uses a minimum amount of spray. If your garden is larger you may want a small tank sprayer or one that attaches to a hose.

INSECT AND DISEASE CONTROL

There are a number of easy ways to avoid garden problems:

- Keep your perennials healthy and vigorous, and leave plenty of space around them for proper air circulation. Overcrowded, undernourished plants are more likely to have trouble.
- Avoid species that are particularly vulnerable to pests. Check the detailed description of each variety you are considering for more information on plant pests and diseases.
- Diseases and insects often overwinter in old leaves and stalks, so cut the stems off every plant in late fall (leave about 2 inches of stubble), and remove them from the garden.

WEED CONTROL

Controlling weeds is an exercise in persistence. If you spend a few minutes each day, or even twice a week, in your garden attacking the weeds, they will be unable to get a foothold and reproduce. Deep, rich, loose garden soil makes weeds easy to pull before they become well anchored, and a mulch discourages the sprouting of seeds that have been scattered by plants in the area, or blown in from afar.

Some gardeners prefer the chemical approach to weed control by relying on herbicides. In the past half century a great many weed killers have been developed; gardeners were told that chemicals would solve all their weed problems. But, like insecticides, some herbicides cause more problems than they solve, and the long-term effects of their accumulation in the soil and groundwater are still unknown.

If you decide to use chemicals for some of your weed control, however, it is important to understand how they work. Herbicides are selective or nonselective. The selective types kill only certain weeds or grasses and are commonly used on farm crops. The nonselective destroy all vegetation: they are sprayed on driveways and paths, under fences, on rights-of-way, and to "clean up" areas before planting.

Dividing Plants

Each spring, after the perennial bed has become well established, some clumps will need to be split up for a variety of reasons. First, the health of many types of plants will suffer if they become too large. As a plant expands, its outer roots may remain healthy, but the middle portion will become crowded and starved for nutrients, moisture, and light. A plant in such condition is called a "doughnut," and it is easily recognizable because the new, stronger roots and stems are visible on the outside. The roots of Shasta daisies, phlox, and chrysanthemums deteriorate in the center as they grow larger, and others, such as iris and coral bells *(Heuchera),* push themselves out of the ground if they are too crowded. Another important reason for dividing is to control growth. Certain plants spread rapidly by nature, and the clumps must be divided regularly to prevent them from crowding out their companions. A third reason for division is that you get lots of new plants to expand your own garden, share with friends, sell, or donate to a community plant sale.

Perennials vary a great deal in their need to be divided, and after a short period of gardening you will easily recognize when the time comes for action. Most should be separated every two to four years, but some, such as chrysanthemum, *Monarda,* and *Anthemis,* need dividing every spring. Well-behaved species — *Dictamnus,* peony, hosta, and others — may thrive for many years in a clump without showing signs of deterioration.

There is some disagreement among gardeners as to what is the best time of year to divide, but those gardeners who live in the North (zones 3, 4, and 5) usually divide plants in early spring. They are still partially dormant then, so they'll suffer less shock and have a long growing season ahead to become well established in their new location before winter. There are exceptions, however. *Doronicum, Primula, Pulmonaria,* daffodils, and other early-blooming plants are best divided immediately after their flowers have faded. The time to separate peonies, iris, and Oriental poppies is, likewise, after their flowering period.

In warmer areas of the country the general rule of thumb is to divide the spring-blossoming plants after they have bloomed, the summer bloomers in late summer or fall, and the fall bloomers in the spring, with the same exception as noted for peonies, iris, and Oriental poppies

HOW TO DIVIDE PLANTS

Think of division as a simple form of pruning. It is as essential to good perennial gardening as the pruning of a fruit tree is to a productive orchard, but, fortunately, much easier.

Perennials are divided differently depending on how they grow. Most perennials fall into one of five categories:

- *Compact, shallow-rooted plants such as* Primulas. Dig up the entire clump and, with your hands, pull it apart into smaller plants. Pry them carefully so the roots will not be injured.

- *Solid clumps such as* Aconitum, Centaurea, *daylilies,* Dicentras*, peonies, phlox.* When the purpose of your division is simply to make a healthy clump smaller, or to propagate one or two new plants, the easiest way is to cut away sections of the exterior with a spade so as not to disturb the interior. If the center of the clump is unhealthy and dying, however, the entire clump must be dug up and cut into pieces (or pried apart with a spading fork if the roots are intertwined). Discard the weak or diseased section and replant the good portions.

- *Bulbs, including lilies and spring-blooming bulbs such as daffodils.* Dig them up, separate by hand, and replant them at the proper depth. Place any tiny bulblets in flats or transplant beds for one season to allow them to come to maturity before they are planted permanently.

■ *Groundcovers and creeping plants such as* Vinca *and* Phlox subulata. Dig the plants up and cut them apart nearly anytime.

■ *Plants with carrotlike roots such as lupine and* Dictamnus. Dig the entire plant in early spring, and cut apart each section with a sharp knife; if you do it carefully, the injured plants will heal quickly.

WHY PLANTS MAY BE GROWING OR BLOOMING POORLY

■ Clumps are too large and need dividing.
■ Plants are set too deep or too shallow.
■ Plants are too small or too young.
■ Possible damage from frost.
■ Soil is too wet or too dry.
■ Plants need fertilizer or lime.
■ Too much fertilizer or lime.
■ Injury from careless use of garden sprays or weed killers.
■ Injury from diseases such as wilts.
■ Injury from insects, including tiny ones such as mites and aphids, or soil pests such as nematodes.
■ Wilting from hot weather, drying winds.
■ Damage from animals such as moles, gophers, woodchucks, deer, or even domesticated pets!

In the spring you will find buds or sprouts on the crowns of perennials. Leave two to four in each division, as you split the clump apart. If you are dividing later, when the plant has live stems, cut them back by at least 50 percent, so there will be less foliage for the roots to support. Don't worry about the way they look: new stems and foliage will grow.

In order to start many new plants, nurseries will frequently divide a clump into very tiny sections, and nurse them carefully until they reach a healthy size. In a home garden it is unnecessary to make the divisions small, since large ones will grow far better and produce more blooms the following season. Unless the plants are huge most are best divided into only two or three new plants. If you decide to produce a lot of plants instead, you can grow these small plantlets in flats or small pots for a few weeks until they have developed good root systems. Then they can be safely planted in a bed.

Chapter 9

A Dictionary of Flowering Perennials

AVENS *(Geum)*. The *Geum*s are bright spots of orange, red, and yellow in either the border or rockery. They are low growing, usually less than 15 inches tall, and many have flowers up to 3 inches across. They prefer full sun or light shade, and ordinary soil that holds moisture well but doesn't stay wet over the winter. None do well in hot climates, but thrive instead where summers are cool and the winters fairly mild, although even in the best habitat they are often short-lived.

BABY'S BREATH *(Gypsophila)*. Lovely in the garden, as a filler in bouquets, and excellent as a dried flower, the *Gypsophila*s are important additions to any border. The clouds of tiny, lacy, white flowers are familiar to most anyone who has seen a floral arrangement. The taller kinds (3 to 4 feet) fit into the border nicely, and the dwarf varieties are useful as an edging or in the rock garden. They like full sun, lots of water, and well-drained, lime-rich garden soil (the word *Gypsophila* derives from the Greek, meaning 'fond of lime'). They need space to grow to their full size and beauty without being moved because their long taproot does not like to be disturbed.

BALLOON FLOWER

    The best varieties of *Gypsophila* are grafted, and these should be planted so that the graft union is set 1 to 2 inches below the soil surface, to encourage root formation above the graft. Pick the flowers as soon as they fade and the plants will keep blooming. Stake them, if necessary.

BALLOON FLOWER *(Platycodon)*. *P. grandiflorus* (balloon flower) gets its name from the partly opened flower that looks like a small balloon. In full bloom it resembles the campanula, with blue, white, or pink star-shaped flowers on 1- to 3-foot stems. Light, well-drained garden soil and sun pleases them, and a winter mulch is beneficial. They are an excellent border plant, long-lived, not invasive, and easy to care for. Because they always sprout late in the spring, mark the spot so you won't accidentally plant something else there or dig them up by mistake. After planting try not to move them, because their long taproot makes it difficult to transplant them successfully.

They are good cut flowers, but will last longer if their stems are singed with a match before being placed in water.

BETONY, LAMB'S EARS *(Stachys)*. The betonies are European in origin, but hardy in the North when sheltered. Some are grown for their interesting silvery foliage, which makes a nice contrast in the perennial garden, and others for their blooms. They like sun or light shade and are not fussy about soils.

BLANKET FLOWER *(Gaillardia)*. These showy flowers with their large daisylike blooms are a worthy addition to any garden, not only because of their beauty but because they stay in bloom all summer. They are available in annual, biennial, and perennial forms, can have both single and double blooms, and various color combinations of red, yellow, and gold. Dwarf varieties start at 8 inches, but most grow from 15 to 24 inches tall. *Gaillardia*s like full sun, and a rich, warm, sandy, well-drained soil. They are fairly hardy, but appreciate a heavy mulch for winter protection in the North.

BLANKET FLOWER

BLEEDING HEART *(Dicentra)*. Bleeding hearts have been gardening favorites for centuries, and few plants attract more attention when they are in full bloom. They do best out of full sun, which makes them attractive to gardeners with shady spots.

The most spectacular is *D. spectabilis,* old-fashioned bleeding heart (2 to 3 feet tall), which is especially popular because it is beautiful in both flower and foliage. The heart-shaped flowers hang gracefully from long arching stems, and range in color from pink to bright red. Except in shady spots in the cool North, *D. spectabilis* dies down after blooming. *D. s.* 'Alba' has white flowers and is somewhat less vigorous than the pink variety. Plant deep in rich, moist soil, in a spot with morning sunshine and light afternoon shade, to obtain the longest period of bloom. The east side of a building is ideal. Leave plenty of room for the plant to grow — 3 to 4 feet is not too much.

BLUE FLAG *(Iris versicolor)*. See IRIS.

BUGLEWEED *(Ajuga)*. *Ajuga* is an excellent, low-growing ground-cover with attractive foliage and blooms, but unless it is used carefully it can crowd out your other garden plants. Ideal for spots where it can be confined, such as in rock gardens, beneath roadside trees, and in other places where mowing is difficult or where other plants do poorly.

CANDYTUFT *(Iberis)*. *Iberis* is a low-growing perennial, often with a woody stem, and one of the best spring-blooming plants. They grow from 6 to 12 inches tall, forming dense mats, and white blooms that sometimes fade to lavender, cover the plants. After candytuft becomes well established, the plant should not be disturbed. It likes sunshine, rich soil, and frequent watering. Usually planted in the flower border and rock garden, it also looks nice in hanging baskets and window boxes.

CARNATION *(Dianthus)*. *Dianthus* is derived from the Greek for divine flower, and so it is. The carnation is but one member of this large family of hundreds of species, most of which have a spicy fragrance similar to clove, and grasslike foliage. The greenhouse carnation is not hardy enough to be grown in northern gardens, but the types of plants called pinks make excellent border plants and cut flowers. Nearly all are dwarf growing, although some get up to 2 feet tall.

CHRYSANTHEMUM

The plants grow well in rich garden soil with a little lime added, and unless otherwise noted, each species needs full sun, good drainage, and good air circulation. Perennial varieties should be divided each year to keep them healthy. Biennials need replanting every year, and even though they may live more than two years, the second blooming is not usually as good. Avoid mulching, because the stems need air circulation.

CHRYSANTHEMUM. The numerous varieties of plants in this large family take so many different forms and bloom at so many different times that they are invaluable in the perennial border. All are good for cutting, too.

C. x *morifolium,* the garden mum, has long been the mainstay of the fall garden because it blooms for a long time and in many different colors.

Mums need sun and rich soil to flourish. Young plants should be pinched back several times in late spring and early summer to make them bushy and well branched. In zones 3 and 4 all pinching should cease by July first, or blooming will be delayed. In warmer zones, continue pinching until mid-July, or until the plant is well branched and bushy and appears capable of producing lots of blooms later on.

Other than the pinching, garden mums need no special care, except to keep the faded blooms picked for best appearance and longer flowering. To get the best blossoms on the larger flowering kinds, pick off all buds except for one at the end of each stem. All the plant's energy will then go into developing a few big, long-stemmed flowers.

CONEFLOWER, GLORIOSA DAISY *(Rudbeckia)*. This large genus of the daisy family includes annuals, biennials, and perennials, many of which are valuable border plants. They are easy to grow and need only full sun and ordinary garden soil to thrive.

Gardeners often dig up bright black-eyed Susans *(R. hirta)*

from beside the road and move them to their flower border without realizing that they are annual or biennial and will die shortly after blooming. (They are ideal plants for a wildflower garden, however, if allowed to reseed.)

R. hirta gloriosa (gloriosa daisy), with bright blooms in orange, yellow, and red tones, gives the garden a full-of-bloom look in midsummer when other flowers are scarce. They come in double, semidouble, and single blooms. Since the plants are short-lived, they must be replaced every few years. They grow easily from seed and, if started early, bloom the same year.

CONEFLOWER

CORAL BELLS *(Heuchera)*. Large flower borders completely edged with red or pink coral bells are an impressive sight. The leaf clumps of this dainty plant are compact and grow only a few inches tall; the brightly colored stalks of tiny bell-shaped flowers are borne on 15-inch flower spikes. *Heuchera* likes rich, moist soil, full or nearly full sun, and requires some winter protection in northern areas where snow cover is uncertain. They are good rock plants, and a clump tucked here or there along a border is always effective because of their long blooming season.

DAYLILY *(Hemerocallis)*. The daylily has been described as the perfect flower because it grows so easily, multiplies well, is easy to care for, and is not susceptible to insects or disease. It can be used in nearly any landscape plan and comes in a wide variety of heights, forms, and colors. The lilylike shape fits well in a formal border, yet is natural enough to plant along paths, fences, pools, and foundations, and the dwarf varieties are excellent for rock gardens and even under trees. For the more practical gardener, the buds and blossoms are delicious stir-fried, and the roots can be peeled and cooked or sliced into salads.

Each flower lasts only a day. Some open in the morning and fade at dusk, but others stay open until midnight. A few open in the evening and last through the next day. In spite of the short life of individual flowers, the *Hemerocallis* blooming season is longer than for many other perennials. Each plant produces many buds, and since the numerous varieties bloom at different times, it is possible to enjoy blossoms for the entire summer and early fall. As a bonus, if a storm wrecks all the blooms one day, the new flowers that appear the next morning will be fresh and undamaged!

DAYLILY

Daylilies like to grow in full sun, but most don't mind some light afternoon shade. The red and pink varieties sometimes have better color if they are shielded somewhat from the hot afternoon sun.

Daylilies like soil that is fertile, well drained, and slightly acid to neutral in pH. The soil should be loose and deep because their root system becomes very large, and most years they need to be watered during the growing season in order to get the best blooms. They need dividing every six to ten years.

GAS PLANT *(Dictamnus)*. There is no middle ground — either you like or dislike the gas plant and its unusual odor; but either way you must admit it is interesting. Its growth habit resembles that of a shrub because it has a mound of leathery-textured, glossy green foliage.

Gas plants will grow in sun or light shade, but they like rich soil and, once planted, should not be disturbed, since they bloom best only when the plant is well established. They are attractive either as single specimens or in groups of three or

61

more, and have no serious pests. Leave a space of at least 3 feet between them.

The pungent odor that gives the plant its name can be better appreciated if, on a hot summer evening when the air is quiet, you hold a lighted match next to the ripe seedpod and watch it ignite the volatile oils in a flash of light. People with delicate skin sometimes get a rash from this oily substance when they touch the plant.

GLOBE THISTLE *(Echinops)*. These hardy plants with their unusual globelike blue flowers are as attractive to people as to the bees that cluster around them. If picked before they reach full bloom, they make excellent dried flowers.

Globe thistles are easy to grow in nearly any soil, and they can withstand dry conditions better than most other perennials. They like full sun or light shade, and should be divided frequently to keep them under control and in a healthy condition.

GOLDEN MARGUERITE *(Anthemis)*. These golden, bright-flowering beauties grow from 1 to 3 feet tall, have aromatic fern-type foliage, and bear an abundance of medium-sized daisies that range from bright yellow to creamy white in color. They grow well in ordinary soil, enjoy full sun, but often spread so rapidly both by seed and underground stems that they require frequent division to keep them under control.

GOLDEN MARGUERITE

It's a big job, but try to keep the flowers picked so they won't go to seed and start new plants. Seedlings usually are not as attractive as the named varieties and are even more weedy.

A. tinctoria is golden Marguerite. *A. tinctoria* 'Moonlight' is one of the best and blooms over a long season. *A. t.* 'Kelwayi' has exceptionally large lemon-colored flowers and grows up to 3 feet tall. *A. montana,* white anthemis, has beautiful creamy white flowers.

HARDY WATER LILY *(Nymphaea)*. Among floating plants, the water lily is certainly the queen. They grow beautifully in shallow ponds, pools, tubs, or slow-moving streams, and all like full sun.

For frost-free southern gardens, and for inside pools, there are many tropical species, including both day-blooming varieties such as brilliant red 'Director,' 'George T. Moore,' and those that open only at night. These come in a wide range of vivid colors as well as white, and many are fragrant.

IRIS. Iris should be considered an important part of every garden because they fill a void between spring bulbs and summer flowers. But even if they did not fill this need, their beauty is too startling to overlook. Iris take their name from the Greek goddess of the rainbow and come in a wide variety of lovely colors. All have flat, sword-shaped foliage, and a flower form consisting of three outer petals (falls), and three inner petals (standards), which are often upright. Some iris species also have beards, or fuzzy appendages that hang from the throat of the flower over each of the falls. There are so many thousands of bearded iris cultivars that identifying a variety in an inherited garden is nearly impossible.

All iris prefer full sun, but each variety has specific soil and moisture requirements. None of the garden varieties can tolerate a winter in wet soil, and all need to be divided periodically so the roots do not become crowded.

IRIS

Iris were once called by the name "flag," but the term is now used mostly to identify blue flag, *I. versicolor,* a blue-flowering plant, and *I. pseudacorus,* yellow flag, a similar one with yellow blooms. Although both thrive in shallow water, they will grow in moist soil, too.

The discouraging thing about growing bearded iris is the various blights, leaf spots, rusts, rots, borers, and thrips that bother them. Cut off any diseased foliage or borer damage as soon as it appears and, if necessary, spray with a garden fungicide once or twice early in the season. And cut off all foliage before winter to prevent pests from lingering. Problems increase when large masses of iris are grown together, so consider placing other plants among them to make it harder for pests to spread.

I. sibirica, Siberian iris, 2 to 3 feet in height, don't mind a year-round moist place. They prefer an acid soil. They are hardy, easy to grow, and are particularly good for planting in wild areas and around water. In the past the flowers were usually blue in color and rather small, but many new hybrids have large blooms in purple, white, pink, and other colors.

KNAPWEED *(Centaurea)*. Of the hundreds of different *Centaurea*s, only a few are regularly planted in perennial borders. Most varieties came from Europe or Asia, but some have become naturalized (and occasionally overpowering) in North American gardens. The *Centaurea*s like ordinary garden soil, full sun, and are useful additions to the border, wildflower, or rock garden, and in planters. The flowers are long lasting and good for cutting. All are very hardy, easy to grow, and need to be kept under control — prevent the plants from going to seed and divide them frequently.

C. *babylonica* (Babylonian centaurea) has yellow flowers and grayish leaves and grows to 12 inches. C. *dealbata* (Persian centaurea) has pink, white, or red flowers, grows about 18 inches tall, and blooms for most of the summer. C. *macrocephala* (globe centaurea) becomes nearly 4 feet tall and has large, thistlelike yellow flowers that attract butterflies in midsummer. C. *montana* (mountain bluet) grows to 18 inches, and has bright blue spidery flowers for over a month in early summer; tends to spread rapidly. C. *m.* 'Alba' has white flowers.

KNAPWEED

LILY *(Lilium)*. The lily is one of the most loved of all garden perennials. Whole borders are grown of these beautiful, fragrant plants that range in size from miniatures to showy, tall specimens that sometimes hold 20 to 30 flowers at a time. Blooms may be recurved (like the turk's cap lily), trumpet-shaped, upward facing, or hang like bells, and be as much as 8 inches in diameter. They come in every imaginable color except pure blue. Although requirements of the many lily species differ, the garden varieties all demand well-drained soil and a location that won't permit the bulbs to become waterlogged for any length of time. Bloom colors are often best if the bulbs are planted where they will be exposed to full sun, but receive light shade during the heat of the afternoon.

Lily bulbs are more fragile than those of tulips or daffodils, and should never be allowed to dry out. If you can't plant the bulbs immediately, store them in moist peat in plastic bags, and plant as soon as possible. Put a little bonemeal in the bottom of the hole and set each one so the top of the bulb is about 5 inches below the surface of the soil. Apply a small amount of garden fertilizer around them each spring, but be careful not to give them excessive amounts of manure or nitrogen.

Most varieties over 3 feet tall need staking, but it's surprising how rugged their stems are, given the weight of the blooms. Begin to stake the plants as soon as buds form. The stems should not be cut immediately after blooming, but be allowed to die down naturally so nutrients can return to the bulb before winter. Because they are planted deep, most lilies are hardy throughout the continental United States and southern Canada, although the Madonna types should be mulched in the North.

LUPINE *(Lupinus)*. Even though they have gone wild in some places and become rather common, lupines are some of the best garden perennials, especially the brightly colored 'Russell' and other hybrids. They come in brilliant shades of red, pink, purple, yellow, white, and blue, often with bicolor shades on the same 18-inch flower spike that tops the 3- to 4-foot stem. They bloom in early summer and may bloom again later in the season if you don't let them go to seed.

Set lupines at least 2 feet apart because the clumps get large, and, once established, it is best not to move or divide them. Where they are happy, they are easy to grow. Never plant them in a swampy spot — a moist, but well-drained soil is much preferred. They also need full sun, and especially enjoy the cool, dewy nights of the Northeast and Pacific Northwest.

LUPINE

MEADOWRUE *(Thalictrum)*. These plants, with foamy pink, white, yellow, or lavender blooms, are good for the back of the border, the wild garden, or alongside streams and other moist places. They like damp soil and light shade, but most will also grow well in ordinary soil and full sun.

PEONY *(Paeonia)*. Even people who can't get excited about spring violets and forget-me-nots admire the giant flowering peony. In Colonial America, the only landscaping many homes had was a lilac bush and a dark red Memorial Day "piney" near the front door. Gardeners today can choose from the hundreds of new peony varieties that have since replaced the old *P. officinalis* (common peony), which invariably fell apart soon after blooming, and had a strong, unpleasant odor. Some of the modern red, pink, white, and even yellow blooms can be 10 inches or more across, and the shrublike foliage, up to 3 feet in height and width, looks nice throughout the summer and fall.

Peonies deserve the extra care it takes to grow the most spectacular blooms. Begin by buying good-sized plants (3 to 5 eyes or sprouts on each bare-rooted clump) from a reliable firm, and plant them carefully in the right spots. They like full sun, but also grow well on the southeast side of a building where they will get light afternoon shade, but plenty of skylight. Allow 3 feet in diameter for each plant.

Once peonies are planted, don't disturb them. They like stability, and will get bigger and more productive each year. Once every eight or ten years they may need dividing, but certainly not more often unless you need to start new plants, or the old ones begin to deteriorate in the center.

PHLOX *(Phlox paniculata).* When phlox is mentioned, most people think of the tall-growing, brightly colored *P. paniculata* (sometimes called *P. decussata*), known as garden phlox, which

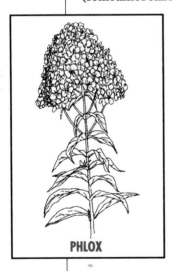

forms the foundation of perennial borders in July and August. But other important members of this family are also worthwhile additions to the garden. Moss pink or moss phlox *(P. subulata)* is only 5 inches high, and it covers banks and rock gardens in early spring with carpets of tiny pink, lavender, red, white, or blue flowers. *P. canadensis,* Canadian phlox (also called *P. divaricata,* wild blue phlox), is 12 inches high and blooms in late spring, covering the plant with flowers in white or shades of blue. *P. carolina* (also called *P. suffruticosa*), thick-leaf phlox, reaches a height of 3 feet and has pink or white blossoms that appear about a month earlier than those of garden phlox.

PHLOX

PLANTAINLILY, FUNKIA *(Hosta).* The hardy hostas produce blue, lavender, or white blooms on long leafless stalks, but the plants are grown as much for their beautiful foliage clumps and because they prosper in shady locations. Hundreds of hybrids have been developed that range in size from small dwarfs to giant-sized specimens, with leaves of all shapes in white, yellow, blue, and variegated shades. Even those who have always regarded hostas as weeds have to admit the colorful new hybrids bear little resemblance to the uninteresting plants of a few decades ago, and thousands of varieties make them a collector's dream.

POPPY *(Papaver).* Like the peony, the Oriental poppy, *P. orientale,* is a spectacular flower in the early summer garden. These long-lived plants grow from 2 to 4 feet tall, on stems that tend to sprawl. Although brilliant orange is their most common color, the huge blooms are also available in shades of red or pink, and sometimes in white or pale pink with a dark blotch. The colors are rather unstable, though, and if you let hybrids go to seed, the vigorous seedlings are likely to produce mostly orange flowers that will crowd out the weaker hybrids.

POPPY

Plant Oriental poppies in full sun and rich soil. If possible, put them in a spot where other plants can camouflage them in midsummer, because after blooming they die down and become dormant, and look messy for a time. New growth appears soon after the old leaves have died, and this is the only good time to divide them, if you want to start new plants.

PRIMROSE *(Primula).* A border of *Primula*s in bloom is a joyous sight. They will reward you if you provide the special conditions they prefer. These cheery, low-growing plants have been hybridized into hundreds of forms, colors, and color combinations.

They like a somewhat heavy, slightly acid soil, which is rich in peat moss, compost, and other humus. The conditions that best suit them are those found in Great Britain and the Pacific Northwest, because they enjoy cool weather and moisture. They thrive in partial shade, especially during the hottest part of the day, but will not flower in deep shade, and are averse to deep cultivation or other root disturbance. Frequent division, perhaps every year, is essential, and should be done directly after blooming. The plants like a deep mulch, and appreciate a covering of evergreen boughs during the winter.

PURPLE CONEFLOWER *(Echinacea).* Coneflowers are a worthy addition to the garden because they offer a large daisy-type, cone-shaped flower in late summer. The plants like a sunny spot, but will tolerate light shade, and grow in ordinary good garden soil. They are long-lived, but need to be divided whenever the clumps get too large — usually every three or four years.

Although the rose-purple blooming species *E. purpurea* (purple coneflower) is the most common, newer cultivars bearing white, red, and pink blooms are also available. Because the plants grow to a height of 3 to 4 feet, they are very much in evidence. The more vibrant shades should be separated from other strong colors by paler shades.

ROSE CAMPION, MALTESE CROSS, CATCHFLY *(Lychnis)*. There are many *Lychnis* species — including annuals, biennials, and short-lived perennials — and several cultivars, each quite different and worth planting in the perennial border. All like full sun, sandy rich soil, and are tolerant of dry conditions.

SAGE *(Salvia)*. The salvia genus not only includes the herb *S. officinalis* (garden sage), and the familiar brilliant red *S. splendens,* (scarlet sage, cultivated as an annual), but also perennial

varieties good for the border that grow from 2 to 5 feet tall with masses of small blue or lavender flowers on long spikes. *Salvia*s are vigorous growers and many have aromatic foliage. They like full sun and sandy, dry garden soil that is not too fertile. Most need winter protection in zones 3 and 4.

SIBERIAN IRIS *(Iris sibirica)*. See IRIS.

SNEEZEWEED *(Helenium)*. This plant's common name arose because the dried flowers were formerly ground into a dust that stimulated sneezing.

The *Helenium*s are closely related to the sunflower, and the blooms are similar.

SNEEZEWEED

They grow from 1 to 6 feet tall, with large flat blossoms of yellow, crimson, bronze, or various combinations thereof, and produce an abundance of attractive, long-lasting cut flowers. They are excellent plants for a large border, and bloom at a time when their colors complement the chrysanthemums and autumn leaves. Most soil types are acceptable, even wet ones; they need full sun, and should be divided every spring for best results.

SPIREA *(Astilbe)*. The *Astilbe*s are a group of feathery-plumed flowers. They range in height from a few inches to several feet, and come in many shades of pink, red, and cream, as well as white. *Astilbe*s grow well in full sun or light shade, in ordinary garden soil. Most varieties behave nicely in the border, although a few of the older types are known to spread quickly and outgrow their spot. They are heavy feeders, so additional fertilizer is necessary if the plants are to thrive. All varieties should be dug up and divided every two to four years.

SPURGE *(Euphorbia)*. This large group of plants contains a collection of annuals and perennials, many of them weeds, and one important flowering shrub, the Christmas poinsettia. The *Euphorbia*s usually found in perennial borders grow from 1 to 3 feet tall, have a milky sap in their stems, and grow best in full sun and dry, sandy soils. Like poinsettias, they have colored upper leaves called bracts (that look like flowers) which surround a small, inconspicuous bloom. Watch them carefully, as they can easily grow out of control.

STONECROP

STONECROP *(Sedum)*. Nearly 400 species are reputed to be in this genus of low-growing succulents. Some are well suited to the rock garden, some are good groundcovers, but others are ugly weeds. Only a few are suitable for the perennial border.

    *Sedum*s are easy to grow. In fact, one of their common names is "live forever." They like dry, infertile soil, and grow in sun or light shade. Their flowers come in a wide range of colors, and one or another is in bloom throughout the season. They are also very hardy.

SUNFLOWER HELIOPSIS *(Heliopsis)*. Another sunflower-type flower, but one that has lost favor because so many similar flowers are better. The 3- to 5-foot plants are sun-loving, hardy, and easy to grow (they will tolerate even poor soils). Resembling zinnias, the large orange and yellow flowers, both single and double, are produced for a long period throughout the summer, and are good for cutting.

THYME *(Thymus)*. The thymes are a remarkable group of herbs and ornamental plants. Their creeping habit and attractive blooms make them perfect, not only for herb and rock gardens, but for planting between stones on terraces, and along paths where footsteps will release their minty fragrance.

Thyme does well in garden soil, but can also grow in poor, dry soil. They like full sun or light shade, and prefer shelter from the wind.

TICKSEED *(Coreopsis)*. Tickseed was so named because its seed resembles a tick, which belies the beauty of its bright, daisylike, yellow-toned flowers. They are a delight in any garden, blooming early and for most of the summer in cool areas. They may self-sow and become weedy, however, although perennial varieties are less troublesome than the annuals.

Coreopsis grows easily in sunshine and moist garden soil. They are excellent cut flowers. The fading blooms should be kept picked to maintain blossoms over a long time. Because they are somewhat susceptible to frost, a mulch is recommended in northern zones.

TICKSEED

WORMWOOD, SILVERMOUND, DUSTY MILLER *(Artemisia)*. Most of these plants have inconspicuous flowers and are grown instead for their unique foliage, which is silvery white, silky textured, and sometimes fragrant. They like full sun, ordinary good garden soil, and an occasional cutting back to keep them looking good.

A. abrotanum, southernwood, grows about 4 feet tall, is shrubby in growth, and makes a nice background plant. *A. absinthium,* wormwood, an old-time medicinal herb, is often planted to repel wild animals from gardens and poultry yards. *A. schmidtiana* (silvermound) is one of the most popular border varieties, which grows into a strikingly beautiful compact clump. *A. stellerana* (beach wormwood, dusty miller), 1 foot tall, is a creeping variety used widely in seashore plantings.

YARROW *(Achillea)*. These easy-to-grow plants with fernlike fragrant foliage have their place in the border, and form nice spots of color, but most species need frequent division so the garden doesn't become filled with them. Species range in size from tiny creeping rock garden plants to 4-foot giants. They grow in nearly any well-drained soil, like a sunny location, and are useful in poor, dry soils.

The hybrid 'Coronation Gold,' (height: 3 feet) is one of the best, with large, golden flower heads which can be dried so successfully that the winter bouquets look nearly as fresh as the summer ones; the plant blooms over a long period. *A. filipendulina* (fernleaf yarrow), 'Golden Plate,' is similar to 'Coronation Gold,' but taller (4 to 5 feet) and with larger flowers. The cultivar *A. millefolium* (common yarrow), 'Fire King,' has rosy-pink flowers and looks best in a wildflower or rock garden.

YELLOW FLAG *(Iris pseudacorus).* See IRIS.

YARROW

PERENNIAL SELECTION CHART

	PLANTING DISTANCE	PLANT HEIGHT	LIGHT	MONTHS OF BLOOM	COLOR	SOIL	pH
Avens	12-18"	15-24"	S	6-8	R,Y	G	N
Baby's breath	12-36"	6-48"	S	6-8	P,W	G/D	N
Balloon flower	12-18"	15-24"	S/PS	6-9	B,P,W	G	N
Betony, lamb's ear	9-15"	8-18"	S/PS	6-7	FOLIAGE	G/D	A
Blanket flower	12-20"	15-30"	S	6-9	R,Y	G/D	N
Bleeding heart	12-20"	12-30"	PS	5-8	P,W	G/M	N
Blue flag	18-20"	30-36"	S	6-7	B	M	N
Bugleweed	10-15"	5-10"	S/PS	5-6	B,W	G	N
Candytuft	10-15"	6-15"	S/PS	4-9	W	G	N
Carnation	12-15"	4-18"	S	6-8	P,R,W	G	N
Chrysanthemum	12-24"	6-36"	S	7-11	P,R,W,Y	G	N
Coneflower, Gloriosa daisy	18-24"	24-36"	S	7-9	Y	G	A
Coral bells	10-15"	12-18"	S/PS	6-9	P,R,W	G	N
Daylily	18-24"	24-40"	S/PS	7-9	P,R,Y	G/M	N
Gas plant	12-20"	24-36"	S	6	P,W	G/D	N
Globe thistle	12-24"	24-48"	S/PS	7-8	B	G/M	N
Golden Marguerite	12-18"	24-36"	S	7-9	Y	G	N
Hardy water lily	24-30"	12-18" ACROSS	S	6-9	B,P,R,W,Y	WP	
Knapweed	10-18"	18-36"	S	6-8	B,P	G/D	N
Lily	30-36"	24-84"	S/PS	8	R,P,B	G	N
Lupine	12-18"	30-48"	S	6-7	B,R,W,Y	G	N
Meadowrue	12-18"	36-60"	S/PS	5-8	P,W,Y	G/M	A
Peony	18-20"	20-24"	S	5-6	R	G	N

	Planting Distance	Plant Height	Light	Months of Bloom	Color	Soil	pH
Phlox	12-18"	24-40"	S	6-8	B,P,R,W	G	N
Plantainlily, funkia	12-24"	18-36"	SH/PS	7-9	P,W	G/M	N/A
Poppy	16-18"	36-40"	S	6	P,Y	G	N
Primrose	10-15"	5-24"	PS	4-6	B,P,R,W,Y	G/M	A
Purple coneflower	12-24"	30-36"	S	7-9	P	G/M	N
Rose campion, Maltese cross, Catchfly	12-18"	12-36"	S	6-8	Y,R	G	N
Sage	12-18"	36-60"	S	6-8	B	G	A
Siberian iris	12-18"	24-36"	S	6	B,P,W	M	N
Sneezeweed	12-18"	24-48"	S	8-9	R,Y	G	N
Spirea	12-18"	24-48"	S/PS	6-8	P,R,W	G/M	N
Spurge	12-15"	24-36"	S	4-6	Y	D	N
Stonecrop	8-15"	6-24"	S	7-9	P,R,W,Y	G	A
Sunflower heliopsis	15-24"	36-48"	S	7-9	Y	G/D	N
Thyme	9-12"	3-8"	S	6-8	P,R,W	G/D	A
Tickseed	12-15"	12-36"	S	6-8	Y	G	N
Wormwood, Silvermound, Dusty miller	12-24"	5-48"	S	FOLIAGE		D	N/A
Yarrow	12-18"	18-36"	S/PS	7-9	R,W,Y	G	N
Yellow flag	18-20"	30-36"	S	6-7	Y	M	N

Light:
s = Full or mostly full sun
ps = part sun or light shade
sh = medium to dense shade

Color:
b = blue, purple shades
p = pink, lilac shades
r = red shades
w = white
y = yellow and orange shades

Soil:
g = general, loamy garden soil
d = dry soil
m = moist soil
w = wet soil
wp = water plant

pH:
N = normal (6 to 6.5)
A = more acid (below 6.0)
L = prefers some lime

Chapter 10

Planting a Cutting Garden

The flower arranger is an artist whose materials are those things that grow around him or her. Choosing and growing your own materials can be as creative an experience as making the finished arrangement.

Successful flower arranging and gardening for arranging take practice and experimentation. But once you have tried it you'll be thrilled to have a work of art on display in your home — your own arrangement.

Growing your own plant material for flower arrangements allows you to plan ahead. With some forethought, you can grow certain flowers for a special event such as a wedding or a flower show, have enough foliage for large arrangements, and decorate your home year round with bouquets of homegrown flowers.

A flower arranger's garden does not, however, have to be large. A garden can be created on a small scale that will give you flowers and foliage throughout the year. Trees, shrubs, edging plants, and even herb and vegetable gardens can be planted with a flower arrangement in mind. Chive flowers dry beautifully and work well in small bouquets. A few leaves of a red lettuce can be tucked into a bowl of green Envy zinnias for a striking, and maybe ribbon-winning, arrangement.

Before planting something you should consider not only how it will look in the garden but also how it will do when cut and brought into the house. In addition, there are other questions to consider when choosing a plant:

- Does it flower?
- When will it bloom?
- What is its lasting quality when cut?
- Is it fragrant?
- Is it available during the barren seasons?
- Does it have a good form or color when viewed up close?
- Does it have interesting branches or foliage?
- Can it be dried or preserved for continuous use?
- Will its color work in the home and with the other plants already in the garden?

At first, this thought process seems odd to some gardeners, but once accustomed to considering plants in this manner, the question, "How will it look in an arrangement?" comes naturally. Not all of the plants you grow will be suitable for cutting. Some flowers won't take up water and will quickly wilt when placed in a vase of water. (Sometimes, however, the container you want to use will be the problem. It may have too slim a neck or not enough space for water.)

In planning your garden you may first want to consider what already grows around your home. If there are evergreens planted near the house, you may have enough foliage for winter arrangements. Perhaps you have lilacs for May bloom and need color in July and August. Or, you have only yellow flowers in a perennial border and yellow is the one color that does not work in your peach living room. Make a list of the kind of plant material you already have and another list of what you would like to have. Then, think about where you could plant this.

Whether you have room for an entirely new garden or just a few new shrubs, the style of your home will help dictate what to plant. Plants selected for containers on an apartment rooftop might be very different from those suitable for a seaside backyard or a country house surrounded by meadows. A city home may want more formal flowers, a seaside cottage may like roses to mix with shells, and a country house may need only foliage plants in the garden to combine with neighboring wildflowers.

Design principles apply to landscaping projects as well as to flower arrangements. Each composition should have the same characteristics: *balance,* a proper size relationship of all the parts to each other and to the composition as a whole, *contrast,* for the sake of interest, rhythm and harmony, and the proper *scale*, or size and proportion.

When selecting plants for your garden, think of these design principles and of the questions previously listed. If you do, the plants you choose will more than likely work well together when picked and placed in that tall Art Deco vase your great aunt Sally gave you. Some plants will work better than others. Don't be afraid to experiment and to change the garden after it's been planted. Some plants, especially in a small garden, will spread too freely and take up space that could be better used by something else.

A small garden for a flower arranger might include a euonymus (either variegated or plain-leafed), a small juniper, a peony, 3 yarrows, 3 astilbes, 2 coral bells, 3 *Heliopsis,* 3 veronicas, a dozen daffodils, and as many zinnias and cosmos as could be squeezed in between the plants. This would, with the help of things gathered from nearby fields and lots, give the arranger many delightful bouquets throughout the year.

But, if you are blessed with space, your problem may not be deciding what to plant, but rather, knowing when to stop planting. It's difficult, especially when there's a flower show on the calendar. There's always something new to try—a new lily, a bicolor cosmos. And, if you do have the room and the strength to keep creating new flower beds, gardening with arrangements in mind can be a never-ending pursuit.

Cutting and Conditioning

Success in flower arranging depends on knowing the best ways to condition and maintain plant materials to keep them looking fresh.

Conditioning is the plant's process of taking on more water than it gives off, so as to put it into a prime state of freshness. It is all-important for creating flower arrangements that will last for more than a day. It is silly to spend all the time it takes to make a lovely arrangement only to have it begin wilting after a few hours because the material wasn't properly conditioned.

The general rules for conditioning most flowers are the same, but there are specific things to do for various blooms. One rule is certain, however: it is best to cut plant material in the evening, because sugar has been stored in the plant tissue all day. The next best time to cut is early morning, and the poorest time is in the middle of the day. This means you have to plan ahead.

Flowers should be cut with a sharp knife or a good pair of garden clippers. Cut the stem on a slant and remove all unnecessary foliage. As soon as the flower is cut, place the stem up to its neck in a bucket of warm water and place the flowers in a cool room for at least 6 hours or overnight. A darkened room will slow the development of the blooms. Any that you want to open should be placed close to an indirect light source.

Some stems need special treatment. Brittle stems (such as on chrysanthemums) should be broken to expose a greater surface for water intake. Woody stems (such as lilac) should be peeled back and split an inch or so. Milky stems (such as poppies) must be sealed with a match or other flame, or by dipping the end momentarily into boiling water. Milky stems need to be resealed each time they are cut, so they are not suitable for needlepoint holders, which pierce the stem.

Some commercial chemical preparations added to the water in which plants are conditioned have value in that they check maturing, nourish plants, sweeten the water, and help slow decay. Other tips to keep in mind are: remove the pollen from self-pollinating flowers; cut the stems under water to keep air bubbles from entering (important with roses); put water in the container before you start the arrangement; and cut the stems straight across for needlepoint holders, and on an angle for deep vases.

Many books have detailed lists of different plant materials and how best to condition them for arranging. The following chart will get you started.

Conditioning Flowers

Flower	When to Cut	Treatment for Conditioning
Anemone	½ to Fully Open	Scrape Stems
Aster	¾ to Fully Open	Scrape Stems
Azalea	Bud to Fully Open	Scrape and Crush Stems
Bachelor's button	½ to Fully Open	Scrape Stems
Bleeding heart	4 or 5 Florets Open	Scrape Stems
Calendula	Fully Open	Scrape Stems
Carnation	Fully Open; Snap or Break from Plant	Scrape Stems
Chrysanthemum	Fully Open; Break Off	Scrape or Crush Stems
Daffodil	As Color Shows in Bud	Cut Foliage Sparingly and Scrape Stems
Dahlia	Fully Open	Sear Stems in Flame
Daisy	½ to Fully Open	Scrape Stems or Sear in Flame
Delphinium	¾ to Fully Open	Scrape Stems, Break Off Top Buds
Gladiolus	As Second Floret Opens	Scrape Stems
Iris	As First Bud Opens	Leave Foliage, Scrape Stems
Lilac	½ to Fully Open	Scrape and crush Stems; Put Wilted Branches in Very Hot Water for 1 Hour
Lily	As First Bud Opens	Cut no More Than ⅓ of Stem
Marigold	Fully Open	Scrape Stems
Peony	Bud in Color or Fully Open	Scrape or Split Stems
Poppy	Night Before Opening	Sear Stems; a Drop of Wax in Heart of Flower Keeps it Open
Rose	As Second Petal Unfurls; Cut Stem Just Above a 5-Petal Leaf	Scrape stems; Cut Stems Again While Holding Under Water
Tulip	Bud to ½ Open	Cut Foliage Sparingly, Scrape Stems, Stand in Deep Water Overnight
Zinnia	Fully Open	Sear Stems in Flame